Using Pro Tools in Music Education

Using Pro Tools in Music Education

Robin Hodson

HAL•LEONARD®

Hal Leonard Books
An Imprint of Hal Leonard Corporation
New York

Published in 2010 by Hal Leonard Books
An Imprint of Hal Leonard Corporation
7777 West Bluemound Road
Milwaukee, WI 53213

Trade Book Division Editorial Offices
33 Plymouth Street, Montclair, NJ 07042

Printed in the United States of America

Book design by Kristina Rolander

Library of Congress Cataloging-in-Publication Data

Hodson, Robin.
 Using Pro Tools in music education / Robin Hodson.
     p. cm.
 ISBN 978-1-4234-9269-6
 1. Pro Tools. 2. Digital audio editors. 3. Music--Instruction and study--
Outlines, syllabi, etc. I. Title.
 ML74.4.P76H64 2010
 780.71--dc22

                          2010048699

www.halleonard.com

Acknowledgments and Special Thanks

My thanks to all the folks at Avid (especially the Sibelius, M-Audio, and former Digidesign groups, both in the education division (Lee Whitmore and Mark Altekruse), and the training division (Carolyn Lightner and Andy Cook). Also thanks to all my new friends at Korg USA/SoundTree.

Special thanks for technical support and assistance from Scott Church and Marc Schonbrun, who patiently answered every question I had. Thanks also to Marc for proofreading these materials.

Thanks to Richard McCready from River Hill High School in Howard County, Maryland, for his faithful support, suggestions, and guidance throughout this project, as well as the music staff (Jim Boord, Shane Jensen, and Tony Domenico), who prompted the creation of this book.

Various members of TI:ME (Technology Institute for Music Educators) have also been very helpful, including Tom Rudolph, Mike Fein, Amy Burns, and Rick Dammers.

I also received invaluable pedagogical advice from Sandi MacLeod from the Vermont MIDI Project (www.vtmidi.org).

Contents

Modules

Part One

Introduction to Pro Tools

What Is Pro Tools?

Pro Tools (made by Avid) is the leading DAW (digital audio workstation), used for all types of audio and MIDI recording, editing, and mixing. Almost every major record and movie released in the world is edited at some stage on a Pro Tools system. Students who want a career in the music industry should know how to use Pro Tools, since they will encounter it everywhere they go.

Pro Tools works on Windows or Mac computers, and special educational pricing is available. The latest versions are within the Pro Tools 8 family. Current versions require the most recent Mac and Windows operating systems. System requirements are always available from Avid at avid.com.

There are four types of Pro Tools software, depending on the hardware you choose:

- **Pro Tools|HD**—The de facto standard for professional recording. Pro Tools|HD requires a special analog-to-digital, digital-to-analog converter (or A/D-D/A) for audio processing. This internal computer card also allows your computer to do complex audio signal processing and mixing, with hundreds of tracks able to play at once. The card is connected to hardware that you plug your microphone and other audio cables into.

- **Pro Tools LE**—A lower cost version of Pro Tools that works with hardware from Avid called the Mbox, or the 003 Rack. Pro Tools version 8 works with the Mbox 2 line of hardware, as well as the new and improved "version 3" Mbox, Mbox Mini, and Mbox Pro. In a school scenario, student stations might use the Mbox Mini and the teacher station would be more highly equipped with a regular Mbox or an Mbox Pro.

▸ **Pro Tools M-Powered**—This is another low-cost version of Pro Tools software. It's designed for use with a wide range of audio interfaces made by M-Audio rather than Avid. Examples include the entry-level FastTrack USB, the NRV10, or even the ProjectMix I/O, which is a control surface/audio interface that includes its own faders. Pro Tools M-Powered software requires a USB key called an *iLok*. The iLok can be unpopular in schools because it is small and can easily be stolen. It can be secured with a standard computer security cable such as a Kensington lock.

▸ **Pro Tools SE**—This is a free, light version of Pro Tools software that works with certain M-Audio interfaces. It provides less functionality, and does not require an iLok.

Please note: *All Pro Tools software versions require a connected audio interface!*

Setting Up Pro Tools

(Share this with your school's technical department)

Take care to set up Pro Tools carefully, especially in a lab environment, or if necessary, consult your dealer or bring in an expert to set it up for you.

Pro Tools is professional audio software. While the LE and M-Powered lines are very affordable, the software is based on the exact same program that audio professionals use. Pro Tools requires a powerful, recent computer. Make sure you have enough hard drive space and RAM for the program to work reliably. Consult your Pro Tools documentation for steps to ensure that Pro Tools runs properly. This is especially important for Windows-based computers, which handle audio processing very differently from a Mac.

Pro Tools will not launch unless the hardware is connected, so connect all your cables and interfaces first. The interface will be the main source for the input and playback of all audio on your computer, not just when you're working with Pro Tools software. If you have a Pro Tools LE system, everything is installed at once from the Pro Tools LE installer. If you're using Pro Tools M-Powered, make sure that you install the driver for your M-Audio hardware first. Then install the Pro Tools M-Powered software. Connect the interface and the iLok and launch the software.

Check to see that the audio and MIDI driver is installed and working, and be sure to test it carefully before you power up Pro Tools. For Windows computers, go to Control Panel > Sounds and Audio Devices to check that the Pro Tools interface is the default device for audio input and output. For Apple computers, go to Apple > System Preferences > Sound and do the same.

Ensure that the hard drive you will be using meets Avid's standards (typically employing a FAT32 file system). Most hard drives should be fine. Some users prefer to use an external USB or FireWire hard drive for all their Pro Tools sessions.

Important Note: Pro Tools cannot write directly to a school network drive. You can archive your work to a network drive later, but while Pro Tools is running, you must use either the computer's local hard drive or a connected external drive. Avid does not officially endorse the use of flash drives (thumb drives). These drives are not fast enough for real-time audio storage, although they are fine for storing copies of completed files, or for transferring files between computers.

Make sure you install all the content that comes with your Pro Tools software. This includes bundled software such as Xpand2!, a flexible software synthesizer instrument; the Structure Free sample player; other virtual instruments; additional effects; and Big Fish Audio loops (these are great for learning how to make and edit audio loops). Look through all the discs that come with Pro Tools and load whatever you need. To use the educational materials in this book, please ensure that the Big Fish audio loops are loaded, as well as Xpand2! and Structure Free.

Pro Tools 8 now checks for updates automatically. As long as your computer is connected to a network, Pro Tools will make sure you're using the latest version and will download the updates for you.

If you're not using Pro Tools 8 yet, you'll want to create an account at Avid (see account.avid.com). Also register your software (go to www.avid.com/activation), since with a registered version you will receive information about updates, and you can usually grab them straight from this page. Pro Tools provides regular CS (customer service) updates such as maintenance releases and bug fixes; please ensure that you're up to date with these as well.

Take a tip from professionals: If it ain't broke, don't fix it. If your Pro Tools system is running well, don't upgrade anything, especially your system software, even if your PC or Mac advises you to do so. Check with your IT department, or call your vendor's technical support line for advice.

On a Mac, try not to run software updates, even if you are prompted to by your machine; these can be harmful to Pro Tools. Instead, run combo updates, which are more integrated software updates, from the www.apple.com website. Search online for the words "combo update apple," and you will usually find them.

On Windows, certain virus protection software like Norton can be extremely invasive to your operating system and will cause Pro Tools not to work. The free AVG anti-virus system may be a more sensible choice instead.

Generally in a lab situation, check with your tech support staff that you have reasonable rights access to the computers so you can log in and download updates with the necessary privileges. If that is not possible, then take your tech staff to lunch and treat them *very* nicely—you will need them during the year!

Technical Support and Training

Your first line of support should be the dealer you purchased Pro Tools from. Avid also provides tech support, and now offers a yearly maintenance contract, which may be a sensible choice if you run many copies of Pro Tools. Consult Avid for more advice.

Online user forums such as the Avid Audio Forums, also known as the DUC; http://duc.avid.com/) are a great source of help if you need quick answers to problems.

The videos that come with this guide will help you in all the main aspects of the software, but if you would like onsite training in your school, or perhaps a webinar with an expert, consult Avid Education or companies like SoundTree (www.soundtree.com)—you'll find plenty of support and help available. A mixture of assistance from the experts and advice from Pro Tools users in the field who are experiencing the same challenges as you are is often the best combination.

Avid also offers official courses and accreditation, but bear in mind that these tend to be targeted quite heavily toward professional users and recording studios. Go to www.avid.com/US/support/training and click on "Services & Training" for more information.

Layout of This Book

The idea behind this guide is to help teachers use Pro Tools with their students, typically in a lab environment.

This requires two basic steps:

> Learning the software (part two of the book)
>
> Creating projects for students to complete (curriculum)

Following a brief introduction to Pro Tools, part two of this book is a step-by-step guide in six sections to help anyone master Pro Tools. You can also use or watch the 41 tutorial movies included to help learn and master the software. These movies should be used later, in the curriculum portion of the book, which is divided into six modules covering the exact same topics above.

Part three of the book is a practical guide for teaching Pro Tools in the classroom.

We want students to understand the process of recording as well as the theory behind it, so they don't just become Pro Tools operators. The idea is to use the software as a tool to aid creativity, and to focus on learning outcomes, creativity, and assessing that creativity.

It is always a good idea to critique students' work and have them listen and comment constructively on each other's work, peer-to-peer. Learning to describe what you hear and making positive suggestions for change is a critical skill for students to learn.

The six lesson modules can be done individually, depending on the time available. We certainly suggest doing Module One, but if time is short, you could skip modules Four, Five, or Six, although you'll be missing a lot of fun and creativity!

Part Two

Teach Yourself
Pro Tools

Getting Familiar with Pro Tools

This part of the book assumes that you have already installed Pro Tools 8 on your computer, and that it is working properly. In conjunction with this section, you should watch tutorial movies #1–6 included on the accompanying DVD. These follow the steps that are being covered.

Pro Tools will work on both Windows and Mac computers, but certain technical specifications are recommended by the manufacturer. For example, you will need a powerful computer with lots of RAM (2 GB or more), and a decent processor speed. More details on the recommended specifications of your computer can be obtained by visiting the Avid website (www.avid.com) and searching for the word "compatibility."

Also, if you are working with a school computer, bear in mind that Pro Tools requires users to be able to save their work onto a local hard drive (typically the hard drive of your computer, or an attached hard drive—not a thumb drive). If your computer is unable to do this, Pro Tools may not launch. You may also have to ensure that you have permission rights to load Pro Tools onto your computer, as well as to run it.

Excellent documentation is available to help you load Pro Tools onto either a Windows or Mac computer, and it is strongly recommended that you create an account on the Avid website.

Before you start, it is a good idea to have some audio available to use in Pro Tools (perhaps from a CD or from iTunes). Sound files on your computer will typically be stored as WAV, AIFF, or MP3 files (also maybe AAC or MP4a files). You will need audio files once you create a new session in Pro Tools.

Each time you launch Pro Tools LE, Pro Tools M-Powered, or Pro Tools M-Powered Essential, the program will search for the required hardware device (typically an Mbox or an M-Audio audio interface), so always make sure that your hardware device is attached and working first; otherwise Pro Tools will fail to run, and will give you an error message. Don't disconnect your audio interface while Pro Tools is running!

If you are using a MIDI keyboard with Pro Tools, it is also wise to connect the keyboard before operating Pro Tools. If you have Pro Tools M-Powered, an iLok will also need to be connected to your computer via a spare USB port.

Some Terminology and Launching a Session

Every time you create a new song in Pro Tools, it's called a *session*, and will have the file extension .ptf. Pro Tools requires you to either create a session or load an existing session before you can do anything else. You even have to name the session before starting work, which is unusual for a piece of software—don't be alarmed!

When you create a new session in Pro Tools, a folder is also created that contains all the important information about your song, such as the actual sound files you've used or recorded, as well as any MIDI information or videos used in conjunction with it. (Soundwaves, incidentally, are always referred to as audio files.) As you create tracks, you can edit them into areas called regions. You can also apply fades to parts of your song. All this information is stored in the same place—your session folder.

After you set the location, don't change where things are being saved—the folder that is created should not be split up or interfered with. If you need to send the session to someone else or move it to a different computer, move the whole folder, not just the session file (.ptf).

1. As already stated, when you first open Pro Tools, no session is loaded, and you will need to create a new session (or load an existing session). The screen should look like this (see **Fig. 1**).

Fig. 1

2. Let's assume you're starting a new session. You will see the following dialog (see **Fig. 2**).

    Give the session a title, save it to the appropriate folder, and click OK. The Pro Tools session will probably look a little like this when you first see it (see **Fig. 3**).

Fig. 2

3. If the Mix window is showing on the front, close that window. If the screen isn't maximized, then ensure that Pro Tools is taking up your entire screen. If you've closed the Mix window, you

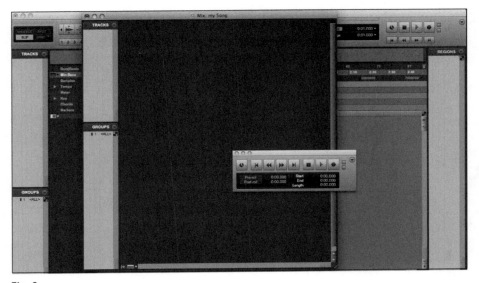

Fig. 3

should now just see the main Pro Tools window, called the Edit window. It will look like this (see **Fig. 4**).

Fig. 4

4. Now is a very good time to turn off a few things and simplify your screen, especially if you are a beginner! First, you'll see a white column on the left-hand side of the screen called Tracks and a white column on the right-hand side called Regions. Neither of these needs to be viewable. Turn them off by clicking on the arrows at the bottom of the screen, next to the white track and region columns. They look like this (see **Figs. 5** and **6**).

Fig. 5

Fig. 6

5. Second, you'll see quite a few *rulers* running along the top of the screen (see **Fig. 7**).

Fig. 7

You might want to turn some of these rulers off, like Samples, Key (signature), and Chords (chord symbols). Go to View>Rulers to deselect these. You might want to leave some turned on, like Tempo and Markers, although if you don't need those, turn them off too until you need them.

6. At the top left of the screen are four important icons called the *modes* (see **Fig. 8**).

   Make sure for the moment that the word slip is highlighted. We will cover more about the modes a bit later. See tutorial movie #4 for information about the modes and what they do.

Fig. 8

7. A little to the right of the mode icons you'll see these icons (see **Fig. 9**).

   These are the actual tools that you'll use in Pro Tools! Three of them should be lit up simultaneously, and these are collectively called the Smart Tools (click on the bar just below the three icons to activate them). Leave it set like this, although you can also click on any one icon to select an individual tool. Most people don't need individual tools however, and for the purposes of this book, you'll hardly ever need to choose anything other than the three tools already chosen. See tutorial movie #5 for more on these tools and what they do.

Fig. 9

8. The icons to the left of the Smart Tools are used for zooming in on things (see **Fig. 10**).

9. **Fig. 11** shows the standard Play controls if you wish to use them.

10. **Fig. 12** shows the Grid and Nudge settings. You don't need to worry about these until later on.

11. **Fig. 13** shows the main display of where you are in a song—notice the white down arrow next to the main number display—click on that, and you'll see that you can express where you are in a song in minutes/seconds (useful for audio editing), bars/beats (useful for working with time-specific data like MIDI or recordings made with a click track), or samples (it's unlikely that you'll need to view this).

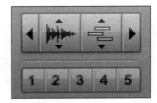

Fig. 10

Fig. 11

Fig. 12

12. This is a small detail, but you
can actually reposition any
of the main icons discussed
above by holding down the
Command key (Mac) or the
Control key (Windows), and
dragging them from side to
side with your mouse. This
way, you can reorder them any
way you like across the top of
your screen.

Fig. 13

Fig. 14

13. Lastly, there should be a big floating window called the Transport on the
screen (see **Fig. 14**).

    If you can't see this, go to Window>Transport to turn it on.

Importing Audio into Your New Session

14. Go to File>Import>
Audio, and look for
some sound files
on your computer
(typically a WAV or
MP3 file). Select a
file, and a dialog like
this will appear (see
Fig. 15).

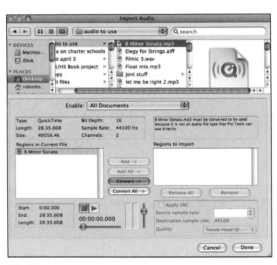

15. Notice the Play icon
button toward the
bottom of that dialog
box—you can audi-
tion the audio before
you import it. Also
notice the blue Con-
vert button—you

Fig. 15

need to click on this to make the audio file "Pro Tools ready." You can also
remove the audio you have chosen before clicking OK, and select something else. If you're ready, click OK. A dialog like this appears (see **Fig. 16**).

16. Don't alter where Pro Tools puts this audio—the Audio files folder is
absolutely fine! Click OK. It'll say "Processing audio" for a few seconds,
and then this dialog box appears (see **Fig. 17**).

17. You probably won't want to change these choices—leave it set to New Track and Session Start—this means that the audio will come into your session as a fresh track, at the start of your session (0 minutes and 0 seconds). Click OK, and your audio will appear looking something like this (see **Fig. 18a**).

Fig. 16

18. There are two sets of soundwaves because it's a stereo recording. Also note that Pro Tools color-codes the track (on the left) in blue. Other kinds of tracks in Pro Tools (like Instrument tracks, which will be discussed later) have a different color.

Fig. 17

19. You should immediately be able to play your audio. The best way of playing audio in Pro Tools is to simply tap the spacebar—no need to click on one of the Play buttons! Tap the spacebar again to stop playing the audio. At this point Pro Tools will most likely play the track from the very beginning (0 minutes and 0 seconds). If for some reason Pro Tools isn't playing the song from the beginning, you can always click on the "return to start" button in your main transport window, which looks like this (see **Fig. 18b**).

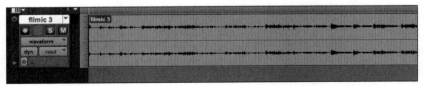
Fig. 18a

At this point, obviously check that you are actually hearing the audio okay—remember, it will be playing through your audio interface (not through the conventional soundcard output of your computer), so you need to have speakers or headphones connected to the output of your audio interface. Adjust the volume controls. If you have an Mbox, for example, you can use the headphone output on the front of the Mbox or the two

Fig. 18b

1/4-inch monitor outputs on the back. Adjust either the headphone or monitor output controls on your Mbox accordingly.

If you get any error messages from Pro Tools at this point, for example that it is unable to play the audio or doesn't have enough memory, there are a few settings you can adjust to improve playback performance (Pro Tools will usually suggest these). The settings can be found in Setup>Playback Engine (see Fig. 19).

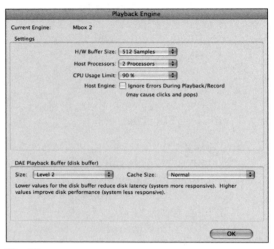

You can adjust the hardware (H/W) buffer size, the CPU usage limit, and (further down in that dialog box) the DAE Playback Buffer size (DAE =

Fig. 19

Digidesign Audio Engine). Level 2 is most likely the default. The hardware buffer size will probably make the biggest difference—think of this as the "pipe" through which the audio is flowing.

The smaller the number of samples, the poorer the quality of the audio will be. The higher the number, the more the audio quality may improve, but it may also use more of your computer's resources. If you experience crackly or stuttering playback (even after changing these settings), you may need more RAM installed on your computer, or a more powerful computer in general.

Viewing, Zooming, and Selecting Audio

1. For this section, ensure that you're in Slip mode, and also that the Smart tool is selected (see above).

2. Once you've played a little of the audio, let's move it around a little. Since your audio file may be longer than your screen can display, you can use the scroll bar at the bottom of the screen to move through the track with your mouse.

3. One other setting you might wish to turn on at this point, which *isn't* always on by default, is automatic scrolling through the audio as your track plays—you'll probably want Pro Tools to continue to display where it is in the audio track when it reaches the end of the viewable screen. Go to Options>Edit Window Scrolling>Page to activate this feature.

4. Notice the minutes and seconds ruler at the top of your screen—below the icons, but above the soundwaves. It displays where you are in the audio. Let's play the audio from a point other than the very beginning. If you have the Smart tool activated, as you hover your mouse over the audio, its appearance will alter between being a hand (when you're over the lower part of the audio) and a regular cursor (when you're over the upper part of the audio). Use the regular cursor to make a selection. Once you've done this, there will be a blinking cursor where you selected, and the main display transport will show you the time point you selected.

5. Press the spacebar to play your audio. Note that when you press the spacebar again to stop playback, Pro Tools returns to where you were.

6. You can also click and drag your mouse to select a portion of audio (see **Fig. 20**).

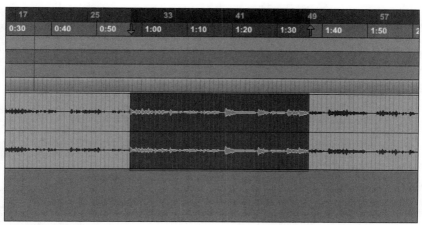

Fig. 20

7. If you then press the spacebar, Pro Tools will only play back the selected section.

8. A word of warning: The Smart tool becomes a Trim tool automatically if you hover your mouse over the very beginning or end of an audio track—this is for trimming the ends of audio, and should be used very carefully (in fact, there are often better ways of trimming your audio than with the Trim tool)! If you make a mistake, and Pro Tools seems to trim your audio, you can always type Command + Z (Mac) or Control + Z (Windows) to undo any actions you perform in error.

9. You can also activate Loop Playback (where Pro Tools plays your selection in an endless loop) by going to the Options menu and choosing Loop Playback (or learn the shortcut

Fig. 21

Command (Command)+ Shift + L (Mac) or Control + Shift + L (Windows). You'll know that loop playback is activated because the Play icon on your main transport window will change to look like this (see **Fig. 21**).

10. Now let's zoom horizontally and vertically on the audio to make it bigger or smaller (this is critical if you want to start working quickly in Pro Tools). On the far left of the track, where the track name is highlighted in blue, you'll see a down arrow just to the left of the track name (see **Fig. 22**).

Fig. 22

11. Click on this arrow, and you'll see different options for the height of the track (see **Fig. 23**).

12. Experiment with the different settings; you might want a larger size. There is also a shortcut for performing this action. Select the audio first (make sure your mouse cursor looks like a hand), and click on the waveform in your audio track. Then on a Mac hold down the *Control* key (not the Command key), and tap the up or down arrows on your computer keyboard. For Windows, hold down the Start key (the name of the key with the Windows icon, usually found between the Control and the Alt keys) and use the up/down arrows.

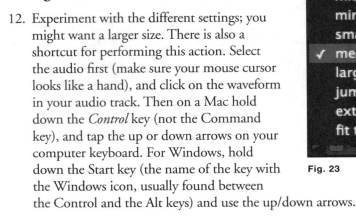

Fig. 23

13. You can zoom in horizontally on the waveform, too: first, make sure the audio is selected/highlighted. Then on a Mac, hold down Command (⌘) and tap either of the square brackets next to the P key: [or]. For Windows, use the Control key and the square brackets.

You can zoom to a very high resolution if you need to, which is great for editing. Don't forget to zoom back out! You can see just how much you have zoomed in horizontally by looking at the minutes and seconds timeline—you can actually zoom all the way in to a thousandth of a second.

14. There are also various Zoom buttons at the top of the screen (see **Fig. 24**).

The left and right arrows on either side of these icons will allow horizontal zooming.

Fig. 24

You'll also see five preset or memory numbers.
Experiment to see what they do—they are actually programmable (refer to the complete Pro Tools reference guide for more detail). The shortcuts to use these five preset numbers are as follows.

Mac: Hold down the Control key and type 1, 2, 3, 4, or 5

Windows: Hold down the Start key and type 1, 2, 3, 4, or 5

Use the numbers above the QWERTY keyboard.

Two other icons you'll see in Fig. 24 allow you to zoom in on the waveform without changing the track height, and there's also an option to do the same for MIDI data (which we don't currently have in our session).

15. Now you've learned how to zoom in and out of the audio, and play it back from any position. You should also be able to freely drag the audio from left to right. Hover your mouse over the waveform until a small hand appears, then drag to the right or left to move the audio in your timeline. Make sure *Slip* is highlighted in the mode box in the top left corner of the Pro Tools screen before you do this—when Slip mode is activated, you can freely move the audio as much or as little as you like around the timeline of your song. We'll start editing the audio in the next section.

16. You can always *rename* your track by double-clicking on the track name on the far left, where it is highlighted in blue. Change the name and click OK.

Other Playback Shortcuts

When you are playing back your track, get into the habit of *not* using the spacebar; instead, use the numeric keypad on your computer for all your transport-style controls.

Use the following keys on your numeric keypad on the right-hand side of your computer's QWERTY keyboard:

Stop	Numeric Keypad 0
Play	Numeric Keypad 0
Rewind	Numeric Keypad 1
Fast Forward	Numeric Keypad 2
Record	Numeric Keypad 3

If you happen to be running Pro Tools on a laptop without a numeric keypad, you have two choices. You could run out and buy a USB numeric keypad, or you can use the Function key on your computer and then type M, J, K, or L to replicate the steps suggested above. Notice that on most laptops, the keypad is embedded in those particular letters—you'll see a 0, 1, 2, and 3 just below those respective keys on your laptop. Note that some newer Mac laptops no longer have this option.

Using the Mix Window

If you don't hear the track playing, now is a good time to check out your Mix window, which controls the volume for all the tracks in a Pro Tools session.

Choose Window>Mix at the top of the screen to open the Mix window, or learn the important shortcut Command (⌘) and the = button on a Mac (Control = is the shortcut in Windows). This will open or close your Mix window—practice the shortcut! It shouldn't cause the Edit window to disappear, but if you stop seeing the main Edit window for some reason, you can get it back by going to Window > Edit.

In the Mix window, your audio track should have a long "strip" with a fader at the bottom (see **Fig. 25**). Halfway down, it says *In* and *Out*. (Hopefully it'll say *In 1-2* and *Out 1-2*.) Press your mouse on each button to expand your choices.

Your outputs are chosen automatically, and there's no need to alter them. The fader will affect the overall volume level of the audio. You will also see S (solo), M (mute), and panning (left/right placement) controls. Believe it or not, there are more effective ways of controlling the volume of your tracks than simply moving the fader up and down—these will be covered in the next section.

Even with the Mix window open, you can play your track. If you have forgotten where you are in the track, close the Mix window (remember the shortcut), click the place in the song you want to play from, open the Mix window again, and press the spacebar to play or stop your song. You can also open and close the Mix window while your song is playing.

Customizing the Mix Window

This might only become important later when you're ready to create a mix of multiple tracks at

Fig. 25

once, but be aware that you can control what you see in the Mix window.

1. In the main Pro Tools menu, go to View>Mix Window Views, and you'll see an array of choices. Most beginners to Pro Tools don't necessarily need to see inserts or sends (these will be explained later). You can choose whether to display any of these in your Mix window. For the moment, you can leave Inserts A–E and Sends A–E selected, and also the track color. Inserts and sends will be explained briefly in the next section of this guide.

2. Also, if you end up working with multiple tracks in Pro Tools, you can choose View>Narrow Mix, which will make each track in your Mix window take up less space.

3. If you look at the Mix window itself, you'll notice a white column on the left-hand side that lists Tracks and Groups. You may not wish to display this—click the left-pointing arrow just underneath your track name to remove this column from view (see **Fig. 26**).

Fig. 26

Editing Existing Audio

For this section of the Teach Yourself Guide, you should watch tutorial movies #7–14, 16–17, and #36 on the accompanying DVD—these follow the same steps that are being covered.

To begin editing audio, you should have some audio in place in your Edit window for manipulation. We'll reiterate the importance of the tools and modes before we edit some audio.

The Seven Tools in Pro Tools

As explained previously, you can click on the different tools at the top of the screen to experiment with using any of them and seeing the effect they have on your audio (see graphic at right). You can always undo any actions you perform—use the shortcut Command + Z (Mac) or Control + Z (Windows). However, the best tool to have selected is usually the Smart tool.

The Smart Tool

The Smart tool consists of three individual tools combined into one: the Trim tool, Selector tool, and Grabber tool. What makes this tool "smart" is that it changes its function based on where your mouse is in relation to the audio waveform. Even though the Smart Tool combines three individual tools into one, there's no practical reason for using the tools individually. The Smart Tool is clever enough to know what you want to do based on where your mouse is positioned.

The Trim Tool

The Trim tool (which resembles a C-shaped bracket) allows you to mask the audio at the beginning or the end of your waveform, removing silence or noise before you start playing.

The Selector Tool

The Selector tool (which resembles the capital letter I) allows you to select part of your region and cut it out, allowing for retakes and precise edits.

The Grabber Tool

The Grabber tool (which resembles a hand) allows you to reposition a region anywhere you want in the timeline. The effect depends on which editing mode you are in. We suggest staying in Slip mode when editing in Pro Tools. Please note that if you are working with *stereo* audio, the Grabber tool only activates when you are in the lower portion of the audio (i.e., the right channel).

Other Tools

The **Zoom tool** (the first icon in the tool palette) is not really recommended, as there are much better methods for zooming that have already been detailed.

The **Scrub tool** is useful when you want to find out exactly where you are in an audio track. Select the tool, then click and drag your mouse quickly or slowly over the audio—you'll see that it sounds a bit like rewinding or fast-forwarding a reel-to-reel tape recorder—you can listen at various speeds to what is going on in your audio at any given point. More advanced uses of the Scrub tool can be found in the Pro Tools Reference Guide, if you wish to investigate these.

The **Pencil tool** is actually very useful for specific editing activities—these will be covered below.

The Four Modes in Pro Tools

As mentioned earlier, there are four main edit modes in Pro Tools (see graphic at right). These can be accessed by either clicking on the relevant buttons or by using the function keys F1–F4 on your computer. Two of the modes are used very rarely, if at all, by beginners to Pro Tools:

Shuffle Mode: Use this when you want to chop up audio and not leave any empty space.

Spot Mode: Use this for precisely editing and moving audio and MIDI data.

You would more commonly use these modes:

Slip Mode: Think of this as your "standard" mode to be in all the time.

Grid Mode: Use this when you want to "snap" regions to a predefined position, usually based on bars and beats. You can use it for synchronizing audio and MIDI data so they line up.

Working with Audio Regions

When you first import or record audio, it creates a single region. If you edit it, add other audio, or in general chop up your track, extra regions will be created.

1. Take your existing audio track, select a point with your cursor, and type Command + E (Mac) or Control + E (Windows). You will notice immediately that the new region has been named in the top left-hand corner.

2. You can now drag that region to the right using your Grabber (hand) tool.

3. You can create as many regions as you like if you are planning to chop up something like dialogue or edit your audio into sections to work on. You can view all the regions in your song and easily access them at any time by locating the small icon in the bottom right corner of your Pro Tools screen. Click there, and the region list appears. Click on any of the regions in that list, and all the audio in that region is highlighted.

There's an important benefit to using regions. If you decide to temporarily not use a region, you can delete it from the track, but it will *not* be deleted from your session forever! You can retrieve it later or use it again—this is ideal for a vocal chorus that you want to repeat later in your song without having to re-record it. Regions are very easy to copy and paste back into your track: just click and drag them from your region list.

Deleting and Making Copies of a Region

The shortcut for copying anything in Pro Tools is Option + R (Alt + R in Windows). So, taking the current audio you are editing, let's say you liked a particular part of it and wanted just that to be repeated.

1. Make a selection, and cut the audio into different regions.

2. Select any audio you don't want (using the Smart Tool with the Hand/ Grabber part of that tool), and type Delete to remove it.

3. Then, select the audio you wish to repeat, type Option + R (Alt + R), and choose how many copies you want. Pro Tools will automatically

paste that audio into the next available space on the timeline, with no gaps. Watch out: make sure the audio loops together nicely—it's essential to make cuts/edits at exactly the right place in the audio.

This is another reason why zooming in is so important: sometimes you will need to zoom in close enough to find exactly where you wish to cut. If you zoom in far enough and display the track height high enough, you can find what is called the *zero crossing point* in the soundwave—0 dB on the horizontal axis. This is an ideal place for making a cut, as you avoid any clicks or glitches in the audio on playback.

Sometimes when you're working with audio that has been recorded with a click track, and is therefore very time sensitive, you'll want to change from Slip to Grid mode. This will allow you to chop up and select audio on exact barlines and beats—which is essential for your music to line up accurately. You don't want to have to guess where to cut a region in this case. We'll cover more on Grid mode when we work with recording audio and MIDI.

Adding Marker Points in Audio

If you want to divide your recording into sections (such as verse or chorus), placing nondestructive markers is the best way to go.

1. First select where you want to position it in the region by clicking in the waveform—this will place a vertical line in the audio. Then, to add a marker, press Enter on your numeric keypad to bring up the Add Marker box. On a laptop, hold down Function and type Enter. A box appears like this (see **Fig. 27**).

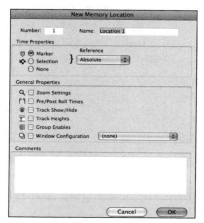

Fig. 27

2. Name the marker point and press OK. Markers will show up in your timeline as small orange tabs.

3. Now you can click on the markers with your cursor to go to an exact marker position in a song. This is ideal for illustrating song structure to students and quickly recalling exact locations in your audio. To move marker points in your song, click and drag them to the left or right. To remove them entirely, click and drag them off the timeline.

Nudging

Sometimes the Grabber tool is not precise enough when you need to move audio very slightly; instead, select the audio you want to move and use the + and – keys on your numeric keypad. Laptop users can hold down the Function key and then use the semicolon (;) and P keys to simulate a real numeric keypad.

The nudge section of your toolbar controls the amount by which the audio moves forward or backward on the timeline (see **Fig. 28**).

Fig. 28

If it's set to minutes/seconds, the audio will move in seconds or tenths of a second, but you can always change the nudge resolution to coarser or finer increments.

Fades and Crossfades

At the beginning and end of your recording, it's common to fade the audio in and out to create a smooth transition from music to silence and vice-versa.

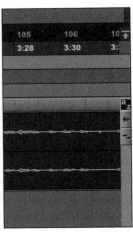

1. The easiest way to add fades is by using two excellent shortcuts: D and G on the computer keyboard. To ensure that these single-letter shortcuts work in Pro Tools, locate the tiny orange-and-black icon that says AZ in the top right-hand corner of the audio waveform (in the main Edit window) and highlight it (see **Fig. 29**).

Fig. 29

2. To add the fade itself, start with a fade in (this obviously happens at the start of any region). With the Smart tool activated, click on your audio track a few seconds after the start of your audio—the cursor should flash. Then type the letter D. You should get something that looks like this (see **Fig. 30**).

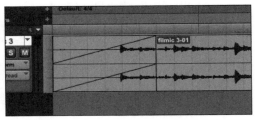

Fig. 30

3. Try adding a fade at the end of any region by clicking in the waveform a few seconds before the end, and typing the letter G. You should get something that looks like this (see **Fig. 31**).

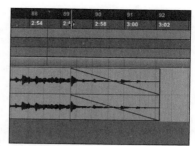

4. Listen to see if the fade works. To delete a fade, simply select the section where the fade happened (just that area should be selected) and hit Delete. Pro Tools won't delete the audio—it will just delete the fade.

Fig. 31

Now import a second track of audio into your Pro Tools session (follow the steps outlined in the beginning of this guide for importing audio). Once this is done, use the Hand/Grabber tool (part of the Smart tool) to drag the new track to just before the end of your previous audio track.

Your session should look like this (see **Fig. 32**).

Fig. 32

If you have a fade at the end of the first track, select and delete it. You can use the same D and G shortcuts outlined above, but there is a slightly better and more powerful way of doing this called *crossfading*:

1. Make a selection across *both* tracks by clicking and dragging with your mouse cursor (the Smart tool must be turned on as usual). The session should look like this (see **Fig. 33**).

2. Now the task is to fade out one track and fade in the other track so it sounds like a smooth transition, like you might hear a DJ or radio station play. Use the shortcut Command + F (Mac)

Fig. 33

or Control + F (Windows), and the following dialog box appears (see **Fig. 34**).

3. You can choose different types of fades. Press OK, and your fade is automatically created. Listen to the fade by clicking just before the fade starts and hitting the spacebar to play/stop your session. You can always undo what you just did and repeat the same steps to try another fade.

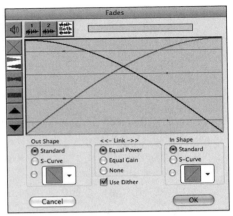

Fig. 34

Basic Automation of Audio Volume Levels

You might think the easiest way of controlling audio volume levels is to open the Mix window and move the faders up and down on each track by dragging them with your mouse. This is generally true if there's only one change you need to make, but when it comes to more complex changes, or songs where you need to vary the volume level a lot, it would be a tough task to wait until your final playback to remember to do all of that—this is how mixes were done in pre-digital days, but life is easier now thanks to something called *automation*. In essence, you can write all your volume changes into the song, Pro Tools will remember them, and all the guesswork of mixing is removed!

To try this, let's work on one of the audio tracks in your session. Incidentally, this whole technique is somewhat separate from fading audio up and down at the beginning or end of a region—think of that as a separate task. What we're working on right now is adding volume changes in the middle of a track.

1. First, go to the left-hand side of the track, near where you see the blue color bar, and you will see the word *waveform* displayed. Click on the down arrow that you see there, and the following submenu is displayed (see **Fig. 35**).

Fig. 35

2. Choose the word *volume* instead, and you'll see that the track now has a solid horizontal line running through it like this (see **Fig. 36**).

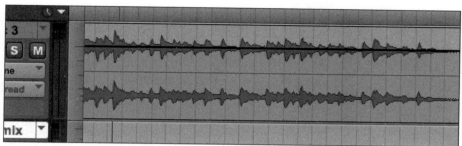

Fig. 36

3. This is the volume line, and the track fader's movement in the Mix window is controlled by whether this line moves or not.

4. Choose the Pencil tool instead of the Smart tool (this is one of the very few times you need to switch to a different tool) (see **Fig. 37**).

Fig. 37

5. You should now be able to click on the volume line and start drawing different volume points in your audio track. The choices you make will obviously be based on musical judgments—perhaps the track gets too loud at certain points, or you simply want to drop or boost the volume at a certain point. When you've drawn in a few points with the Pencil, your track may look something like this (see **Fig. 38**).

6. You can even draw in a whole series of volume changes by clicking and dragging with the Pencil tool, but this is not

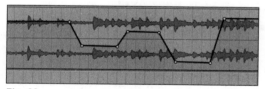

Fig. 38

normally necessary. Usually just some discrete marker points are fine. As soon as you're done, turn the Smart tool back on—you'll need it again.

7. Play the track from before where you put the volume changes in. While it is playing, open the Mix window, and watch your fader in the Mix window move all by itself. Congratulations—you just wrote your first bit of automation!

If you start writing volume changes into all of your tracks in a multitrack session, you can imagine how much easier creating a final mix becomes.

A reminder, in case it hasn't been obvious: whenever you want Pro Tools to play at the very beginning of a session, select the Return to Start icon on the main floating Transport window (mentioned earlier):

Fig. 18b

You can repeat any of the fades and volume changes/automation you just learned on any region in any session you create. These are very important skills to learn that will enable you to work fast in Pro Tools.

One final piece of advice: Once you've finished drawing volume automation in a region, you may want to go back to viewing the track as a normal waveform. Choose waveform instead of volume in the far left of the track, near the blue color bar).

Cutting a Region Using Shuffle Mode

Occasionally you may want to cut out unwanted noise in a region, but not leave a gap (this is something used most often with voiceovers or speeches). As you should know by now, you can certainly chop a region up into many different subregions using the shortcut Command + E (Mac) or Control + E (Windows), as shown in **Fig. 39**.

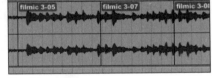

Fig. 39

You can select any of these and delete them, which will create a gap that looks like this (see **Fig. 40**).

Perhaps there's a quicker way of removing what you don't want and not leaving a gap at all? There is.

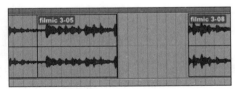

Fig. 40

1. Choose a region to work on, and make a selection by clicking and dragging so it looks like this (see **Fig. 41**).

2. Because you have selected more than just a single point in the audio, when you cut this region up using the usual shortcut Command + E (Mac) or Control + E

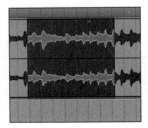

Fig. 41

(Windows), Pro Tools understands and creates a whole separate region for your selection.

3. Now turn on Shuffle mode in the top left (this is almost the only time you might do this).

4. With Shuffle mode turned on, press Delete to remove your selected region, and you'll notice that no gap has been created—Pro Tools has joined the two regions that were on either side of your selection. Be careful, of course, because this can sound strange on playback! It is a useful feature, though. As soon as you are done with this, return to Slip mode, which is the default mode that Pro Tools should be using.

Joining Separated Regions

This is a small but sometimes useful thing to know, especially when you are editing your audio and it has lots of regions that are becoming unwieldy. Can you effectively glue all the regions back together? This is called *heal separation* in Pro Tools, and is easy to do with a shortcut.

1. First, select several regions. This is perhaps easiest done (with the Smart tool) by clicking on one region and shift-clicking on another region, so two or more are selected like this (see **Fig. 42**).

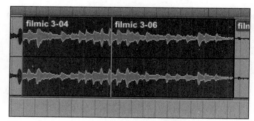

Fig. 42

2. Now type Option + Shift + 3 (Mac) or Alt + Shift + 3 (Windows). Make sure both Option/Alt and Shift are held down, and use the 3 that is above the W key on the main computer keyboard. This should join the regions together into one.

Fig. 43a

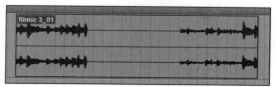

Fig. 43b

3. You can also do this to join regions together if there is a gap in between them. **Figs. 43A** and **43B** show before and after shots.

Stretching or Contracting Audio Using the Time Compression/Expansion Tool

Tutorial movie #16 also covers this topic.

While Pro Tools provides advanced ways to alter the timing of audio, called Elastic Time (see later in this guide for more on this, as well as tutorial movie #18), the simple way to alter the length of an audio region is by using the Time Compression/Expansion tool, or TCE.

1. First, choose the audio region you want to work on. At this point, either of the two main modes in Pro Tools (Slip mode or Grid mode) would be appropriate to have turned on, although each may affect the outcome differently. Select the Time Compression/ Expansion (TCE) tool by pressing and holding your mouse over the first of the three tools that form the Smart tool. The following dialog appears (see **Fig. 44**).

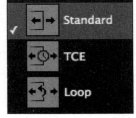

Fig. 44

2. Choose TCE, and your tool selection should now look like this (see **Fig. 45**).

Fig. 45

3. At this point, as you hover over the audio, you'll notice that your mouse cursor has changed its appearance to look like the TCE tool itself. Click somewhere in the audio before the end, and Pro Tools will reduce the length of the audio to where you have clicked. This process may take a few seconds, depending on how long the region is. You can always undo this step using the standard shortcut Command + Z (Mac) or Control + Z (Windows).

4. Try again, this time clicking on the timeline after the region ends, and you'll notice that Pro Tools extends or stretches the audio so that it now lasts longer. It will not alter the pitch of the audio, just its timing.

This can be a useful tool on occasion, especially when used with the spoken word. If you contract or stretch the audio a lot, some degradation of the audio will be noticeable.

If you have Grid mode activated when you perform tasks with the TCE tool, you will notice that where you click with your mouse will *snap* to a predefined grid, and you will have slightly less flexibility in where you can click. This is actually ideal if you are working with time-sensitive material and want your region to be an exact length in seconds, bars, or beats.

Using Pitch Correction in Pro Tools

A little like the TCE tool mentioned above, there is a simple way to alter the pitch of audio in Pro Tools, but its length will also be affected. More sophisticated pitch-correction plug-ins, such as Antares Auto-Tune, allow the pitch to be altered *without* affecting its timing.

1. With the Smart tool selected, select some audio to work on, either by clicking and dragging or by selecting a whole region. You must have some audio selected for the following feature to work. Play it back to check that it is the correct bit of audio that you want (hint: use the spacebar for playback).

2. Now go to AudioSuite > Pitch Shift > Pitch shift, and this dialog box appears (see **Fig. 46**).

3. This is where you can make alterations to the audio's pitch. Note the word Preview on the bottom left. Always use Preview first to audition the changes. Press Preview and the audio region you selected will start playing. Experiment with dragging the sliders that say Coarse and Fine, and perhaps some of the other settings. Press Preview again to stop playback.

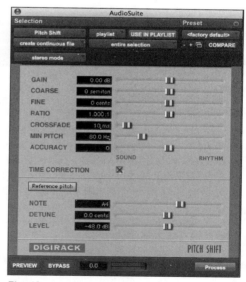

Fig. 46

4. If you want to make a permanent change to your audio, click Process in the bottom right of the dialog box, but be warned: edits like this that you perform in AudioSuite are considered *destructive*, in the sense that

they are basically undoable. If you are not happy with the results, you will have to go back and reimport your region and audio as you did at the beginning.

Making Audio Louder

Sometimes you will find that even after you have raised the fader volume in the Mix window the audio you have imported or recorded is simply not loud enough. Pro Tools provides several AudioSuite tools to assist you, but once again, be warned—AudioSuite processes should be considered *final*, as they cannot be reversed.

1. Select some audio as you did before, with the Smart tool activated. Play it back to make sure it's the right audio. Then go to Audio Suite > Other > Normalize, and the following dialog box appears (see **Fig. 47**).

Fig. 47

2. Notice the slider that allows you to choose the decibel level of your audio. There are also Peak and RMS buttons. Peak will allow you to set the highest volume level of your audio, and RMS will allow you to set the average volume level of your signal. Watch out—choosing RMS and processing your audio can cause it to get very loud indeed! Peak is a better and more normal choice for most audio. Move the slider until it reads –3 dB (the industry-standard volume for voiceovers). Click Process, and Pro Tools alters the overall volume of the audio you selected.

3. Immediately after performing this action, you can choose Undo (Command + Z/Control + Z) to return your audio to the way it was before.

Another way you can alter the volume level of audio in AudioSuite is to go to AudioSuite>Dynamics>Bomb Factory. Pro Tools will then load a peak limiter plug-in that will affect the overall volume level (see **Fig. 48**).

Notice that the plug-in has both an input and an output volume control, which you can change by clicking and dragging up or down. Also note the Preview and Process buttons, and use them accordingly.

Fig. 48

Using AudioSuite in Pro Tools

Tutorial movie #36 talks about AudioSuite—you may wish to watch this in conjunction with this guide.

As stated above, AudioSuite effects are not always the best way to process or alter audio in Pro Tools, because changes are permanent. You will notice that AudioSuite provides a wide range of effects, including EQ, reverb, and delay (very common effects used in recording studios). Explore these by all means, but also read the following section about using *insert* effects instead, which is the more "correct" way of adding effects to audio, and gives you more flexibility in all stages of the editing process.

That said, some of the AudioSuite features we already discussed, like Normalize and Pitch Shift, are better done here than elsewhere in Pro Tools. There are also useful AudioSuite features you should explore, like the Noise Reduction plug-ins, and a few more you'll find in AudioSuite>Other, like the always popular Reverse feature.

Always follow the same steps when processing audio. Save your session first and ensure that you are using the Smart tool, then select the audio you wish to work on.

Many of the effects you choose, like Reverse, will have a Preview button, so you can hear what the audio will sound like before you press the Process button and permanently edit the audio.

One advantage to using AudioSuite rather than insert effects (covered below) is that you will use up less computer memory. Insert effects, if they remain active, draw processing power, whereas running an AudioSuite plug-in can be thought of as a one-off event. Once your audio has been processed, less memory will be used.

Making Copies of Your Audio

Sometimes when you are doing a dramatic effect such as reversing your audio, you might want to make a copy of your region before you start processing it. This is best done by creating a new, empty track in your Pro Tools session.

1. Go to Track > New, or use the shortcut Command + Shift +N (Mac) or Control + Shift + N (Windows). A dialog box appears (see **Fig. 49**).

Fig. 49

2. In this case (assuming you are working with a stereo audio file that you imported into Pro Tools), if you want a copy to be made of some stereo audio, create one stereo audio track. An extra blue track will appear in your Pro Tools session.

3. At this point, (making sure you have the Smart tool activated) you can locate the audio region you need to make a copy of, and select it with the Hand/Grabber.

4. Now hold down the Option key (Mac) or the Alt key (Windows) and drag the audio region into your new empty track. It should simply make a copy of the audio, and leave the original audio in place where it was. This is great for creating a spare version of your audio region for safety purposes. Now you can experiment on the audio you made a copy of.

Deleting a Track Entirely

If you have an unwanted track in your song, the safest way to delete it (and not delete another track by mistake) is to select the *title* of your track (on the far left). It should light up. Now go to Track>Delete. Pro Tools may give you this warning message (see **Fig. 50**).

What Pro Tools means by an "active region" is one that is in use by the current session. Pro Tools doesn't delete regions unless you explicitly want it to. It stores them in the Regions list, which you can

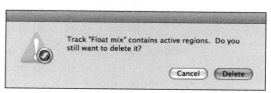

Fig. 50

view at any time by clicking on the arrow in the bottom right of your Edit window (see **Fig. 6** on page 10). You can always recall and drag audio regions back into your session at any time, even ones that you have deleted.

Using Insert Effects Such as EQ, Reverb, and Compression

Tutorial movies #12–14 cover these topics.

Using effects as insert effects is a different approach than using the AudioSuite effects mentioned previously. Although you will find EQ, reverb, compression, and other audio effects there, using these same effects as insert effects gives you much greater flexibility, because you can continue to make changes to your settings right up until you do a final mixdown and *render*, or bounce, your session to a completed stereo audio file.

That said, reverb in particular, as well as delay, is commonly used in tracks a different way than as insert effects—this will be explained later in this guide under "creating an auxiliary send" (also covered in tutorial movie #34). But for the moment, let's look at this way of adding EQ, reverb, and compression.

The curriculum part of this book talks about what EQ, reverb, and compression actually do to audio, and why they are important. Suffice to say that these effects are absolutely critical—just as important as the volume level of a track. They are all used the following way.

1. First, prepare your track. Ensure you have some audio selected. Select a portion of it (use the Smart tool to select part of the region by clicking and dragging).

Fig. 51

2. Perhaps also turn on Loop Playback, which we discussed earlier (Command + Shift + L/Control + Shift + L). Start playing the audio (the spacebar is the shortcut), and you should hear the audio looping nonstop. This is quite useful, because we can now go to the Mix window and start inserting our effects.

3. Open the Mix window while the audio is playing (Command + = or Control + =). You should see that the track's volume is visible as it plays, on the fader (see **Fig. 51**).

4. Now look toward the top of the channel strip. You'll see the section Inserts A-E, featuring five dark-gray slots. Click on the top one, and the following will appear (see **Fig. 52**):

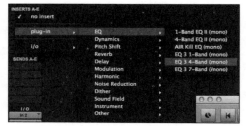

5. Choose Plug-ins > EQ > EQ 3 4-Band (Mono). A new window appears with

Fig. 52

four colored points (called *bands*). You can drag these points up and down and left and right to alter the frequencies of the audio. The blue ball handles the highest-pitched frequencies, all the way down to the red ball, which handles the lowest, deepest frequencies.

6. Experiment to see if you can alter the sound of the music. Your screen may end up looking a bit like this (see **Fig. 53**).

7. Note that there is a button at the top of the floating EQ window that says Bypass, where you can temporarily turn off the EQ changes you made and hear the music without your alterations.

Fig. 53

8. Also note that as you move the colored points up, down, left, and right, that the virtual knobs underneath also move. There is an additional knob you can alter

just with your mouse called the Q. The green one looks like this (see **Fig. 54**).

Adjusting this will alter the bandwidth, or Q, of the frequency range you have been boosting or cutting.

Fig. 54

You can easily spend a long time working on EQ, especially as every track in your song can have its own EQ. The one we chose (4-band EQ) is only one kind of EQ—you can experiment with trying different EQs from the list we saw earlier.

9. Close the floating window when you have finished working on it. The effect will remain active, unless you have hit the Bypass button, or until you remove the insert effect from the insert slot in the Mix window.

10. To remove the insert effect entirely (effectively deleting it), close the EQ window, go to the same insert place in the Mix window where you added the EQ, click just to the left of the name of the EQ, and you'll see a dot. Click on that. Then choose No Insert, and the EQ will be removed (see **Fig. 55**).

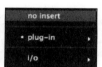

Fig. 55

Follow the same process for inserting reverb. Try inserting reverb on your track.

1. Click on the same insert point and choose D-Verb (mono) (see **Fig. 56**).

2. This screen now appears (see **Fig. 57**).

Fig. 56

3. Notice the second slider from the top—that's the one that controls how much reverb is being added. Drag it all the way to the left (listening to your track as it plays), and you can easily hear the reverb effect.

4. Notice all the other settings in this window, and experiment with them. The *algorithm* and *size* of the reverb will also

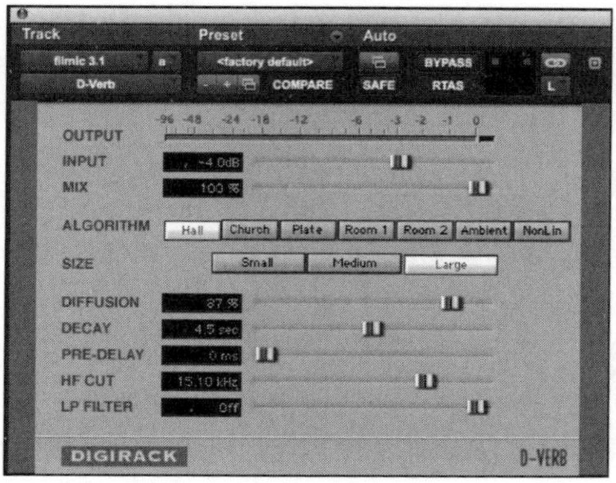

Fig. 57

make a big difference—perhaps try different-size virtual rooms. As usual, there is a Bypass button so you can hear your track without the reverb settings you created. You can also experiment with the presets, which you'll find on the same screen, below the word Preset.

5. Close the floating window when you have finished working on it. The effect will remain active unless you hit the Bypass button, or until you remove the insert effect from the insert slot in the Mix window.

6. Follow the same process for inserting compression:

7. First, remove the first plug-in (click on the small dot next to the name of the inserted reverb plug-in, in the Mix window). Replace it with Compressor/ Limiter Dyn 3 (mono) (see **Fig. 58**).

Fig. 58

8. The new screen you see should look like this (see **Fig. 59**).

9. Compression is a more complex effect in some ways, since it mainly acts on the dynamic range of your audio (the range between loud and soft). The curriculum section of this book covers more on compression and limiting.

Fig. 59

10. Try experimenting with changing all six of the virtual knobs that you see toward the bottom of the screen. Probably the most important is the yellow Thresh or threshold button, followed by the red Gain button, and Knee, which describes the type of compression. The graphical screen (as well as the level meters on the left-hand side) will show what is happening to your audio.

11. Close the floating window when you have finished working on it. It will remain active unless you have hit the Bypass button, or until you remove the insert effect from the insert slot in the Mix window.

Using All the Effects Together

Tracks can have more than one insert effect on them. In the Mix window, Pro Tools allows for up to 10 insert effects, which is more than most people would ever use, but it is not uncommon to use three or more insert effects. The order that you insert them will actually heavily affect the sound; Pro Tools processes the audio from the top down, so to speak, so the audio will be affected by the first inserted effect, then the second, and so on. Of the three effects discussed above (and there are many more to discover, the same way we found the three discussed above), the first insert should probably be compression, followed by EQ, and then reverb. You can actually insert them all, as shown here (see **Fig. 60**).

Fig. 60

You can then move their order by dragging the insert effect up and down with your mouse to see how that changes the sound of your audio.

Other popular effects you may wish to explore include delay, chorus, flanger, and phaser, which you'll find in the Modulation group of plug-ins, and perhaps distortion and fuzz-wah, which you'll find in the Harmonic group.

We will cover more on using effects later (in particular, how to make an effect apply to many tracks at once, using the auxiliary sends) when we discuss multitrack recording.

Working with MIDI and Instrument Tracks

Accompanying this section of the Teach Yourself Guide, you should watch tutorial movies #19–27 on the accompanying DVD—these follow the same steps that are being covered.

Important Information

This section introduces you to two kinds of tracks in Pro Tools—MIDI tracks and Instrument tracks. In some respects they are very similar, but there is one crucial difference, relating to what kind of MIDI keyboard you have connected to your computer. If your MIDI keyboard has no internal sounds (what is called a controller, or silent, keyboard), you will have no use for creating MIDI tracks at all. If your keyboard has sounds (what you might call a synthesizer, or perhaps a digital piano), you can use either MIDI tracks or Instrument tracks.

MIDI Files Explained

MIDI tracks in Pro Tools are designed to play only through an external sound device attached to your computer—typically a synthesizer or digital piano. Pro Tools cannot play back a MIDI file using your computer's internal soundcard.

There are thousands, perhaps millions, of MIDI files available on the Web. There is probably a MIDI version of most famous songs and pieces, and many of these are free to download online.

A MIDI file is a set of instructions for a sound source to play. It does not contain the actual soundwaves. However, some MIDI files—perhaps most—are illegal (copyright law states that a MIDI file of a recently composed song is illegal unless you have paid for the rights).

You can download MIDI files and open them in Pro Tools. If you have a keyboard with sounds, see the next section. If your keyboard has no sounds, or you don't have a MIDI keyboard hooked up to your computer, you can convert the MIDI tracks to Instrument tracks and play them in Pro Tools (see below).

Alternatively, you can, of course, generate your own MIDI (or Instrument) tracks in Pro Tools—but most likely you'll need a MIDI keyboard. It is possible to input MIDI notes into Pro Tools using your mouse, but that is a very slow and painstaking task, especially when a silent MIDI controller can cost you well under $100. It's a good extra thing to have.

Opening a MIDI file

1. See if you can find a MIDI file on your computer (a MIDI file has the file extension .mid). If not, download a MIDI file from the Internet. There are plenty of free resources available. Save it on your desktop.

2. Then, open Pro Tools, start a new, blank session, and go to File>Import>MIDI. Locate where the MIDI file is on your computer, and click OK. The following dialog box will appear (see **Fig. 61**).

3. Check the boxes that say "Import tempo map" and "Import Key Signature." This important information will then be stored and used for playback in your Pro Tools session.

4. Your MIDI file should appear in a new track within Pro Tools. The track(s) will most likely be colored purple on the far left of your Edit window (see **Fig. 62**).

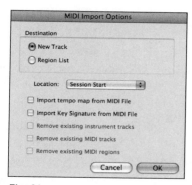

Fig. 61

5. If your MIDI file has multiple tracks in it, each one should now appear in your Edit window. Scroll up and down on the right-hand side of your Edit window to see how many tracks have appeared. Each instrument will probably have its own track. If the tracks already have names, these will appear too. The MIDI data will look a little different from audio, because it doesn't contain sound-waves. It's just a set of in-structions, or *MIDI events*.

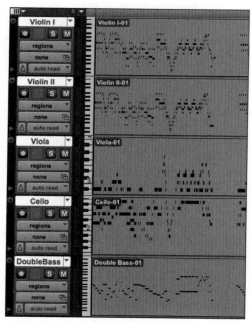

6. The first thing to check is if the MIDI file will play back (you will need to have a synthesizer or digital piano connected for this to work). This is your receiving device— Pro Tools will send the information to the synthesizer on playback. Also, your receiving device needs to be capable of

Fig. 62

receiving information from several MIDI channels at once (many digital pianos cannot do this).

7. If you have no MIDI keyboard attached, or if your keyboard has no internal sounds, no sound will happen at all on playback of a MIDI file.

8. Now look at the Mix window. The shortcut to open it is Command + = (Mac) or Control + = (Windows) (see **Fig. 63**).

Fig. 63

9. You'll need to choose an *output* for each MIDI track, if one isn't selected already. This is found halfway down each channel strip, under the section that says I/O (see **Fig. 64**).

10. The first gray box is the input (not important right now, since no new MIDI information is being input). The lower gray box is the output, which is critical—where do you want to send the MIDI information, and which MIDI channel do you want to use? Bear in mind that there are 16 MIDI channels in total, and if you have a normal synthesizer, it should be able to receive MIDI information simultaneously on all 16 MIDI channels. Consult your synthesizer's user guide if you are unable to set your synthesizer to this mode, which is sometimes called Multi mode or Multitimbral mode. Setting all this up should allow you to play your MIDI file back through your connected synthesizer.

Fig. 64

Looking at MIDI Data

Once you have established an output for each of your MIDI tracks in the Mix window, you can close it and return to the Edit window. You can edit your MIDI data in many different ways. These will all be covered below, when we talk about Instrument tracks, which behave exactly the same way as MIDI tracks from an editing standpoint. The same windows apply when editing both kinds of tracks.

Turning MIDI Tracks into Instrument Tracks

If you have a MIDI file open in Pro Tools, and you don't have a MIDI keyboard with its own sounds, you have to use the virtual instruments inside Pro Tools.

This involves creating new tracks and copying the MIDI data into those tracks. Here are the steps to do this:

1. Open the MIDI file (as described above). All the tracks will appear in purple on the far left-hand side of the Edit window.

2. Count how many tracks there are in the MIDI file, and make a note of the track names, if there is any information about what instrument is featured (i.e., drums, bass, or guitar).

3. Type Command + Shift + N (Mac) or Control + Shift + N (Windows). The new tracks dialog appears. Create the same number of tracks as are in your MIDI file as *mono Instrument* tracks (see **Fig. 65**).

Fig. 65

4. The new tracks will all appear in orange on the far left of the main Edit window. Now scroll back to the top of the Edit window (use the scroll bar on the right-hand side).

5. Make sure the Smart tool is selected. Click on the MIDI data in the first track with your virtual hand, using the mouse (it should all become highlighted).

6. Click and drag all this data downward until Pro Tools scrolls toward the bottom of the page, and "drop" it onto the first empty orange-colored Instrument track.

7. Repeat this step for all of the MIDI tracks—you are literally dragging the data from the MIDI tracks to the Instrument tracks. Sorry—there isn't another way!

8. When you are done, you can delete the old, unwanted, and now empty MIDI tracks (as long as you remember the sounds that each track made, based on the name of each track).

9. Now you need to load up a sound for each Instrument track, using one of Pro Tools' virtual instruments. Read the next section for how to do that.

10. Your song should now play back using virtual instruments.

Creating and Recording Your Own MIDI Tracks

Bear in mind that, as in the previous section, MIDI tracks are only useful in Pro Tools if you have a MIDI keyboard attached with its own sounds (i.e., a synthesizer). If you don't, skip this section and go to the next section on Instrument tracks instead (these are the virtual instruments inside Pro Tools that you can trigger without having a synthesizer attached).

1. To record into a MIDI track, start a new blank Pro Tools session and name it.

2. Add a new MIDI track (Command + Shift + N or Control + Shift + N).

3. Choose one mono MIDI track. It will appear in purple on the far left of the Edit window.

4. You're almost ready to record some MIDI. You might want to create a **MIDI click track** too, so you count bars and beats. Go to Setup>Click/Countoff, and a dialog box appears (see **Fig. 66**):

5. Ensure that you've chosen an output for your click track (so you can hear it!), and make sure the click is on MIDI channel 10 (drums). Obviously also ensure that your MIDI synthesizer is connected, turned on, set to Multichannel receive mode, and that you can hear the synthesizer's sounds.

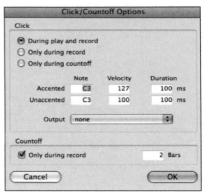

Fig. 66

6. Now choose the **sound** you want for the MIDI track: in your MIDI track's settings (on the right-hand side of the track in the Edit window), you'll see this (see **Fig. 67**).

Fig. 67

7. Click on the word None. This dialog box appears (see **Fig. 68**).

8. You'll most likely see a series of numbers—these represent the sounds in the banks inside your connected synthesizer. If your synthesizer is set to something called *General MIDI*, this is a universally accepted list of sounds. For example, 0 is piano, and 53 is voice (refer to a General

MIDI sounds
list to discover
which sound
uses which
number—there
are 128 to
choose from).

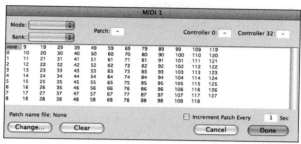

9. Record-enable
the MIDI track
(by clicking

Fig. 68

on the red circle in the track box on the left-hand side, next to the
purple bar). Make sure you're not using Loop Playback (Options>Loop
Playback should not be checked). Press the Record button on the
main floating transport window, then press Play (or spacebar) to begin
recording. You should hear a click track playing if you set up a MIDI
click. Play some notes on your MIDI keyboard. Press the spacebar or
Stop. MIDI data should have been recorded, which you'll see. If you
don't see any new data, check the settings described earlier.

10. To hear back your MIDI performance, first ensure that the main cursor
is set to the Smart tool. Then click somewhere in the timeline (or rewind
to the beginning), and press Play. You can edit and alter all of your MIDI
data in exactly the same way you would with Instrument tracks, so read
on to see how this is done.

Creating and Recording with Instrument Tracks

Here are a couple of useful first steps to do before you start working with
Instrument tracks. Remember that Instrument tracks use the *virtual instruments*
inside Pro Tools (and there's plenty to choose from). You don't need a MIDI
keyboard with sounds, but a silent MIDI keyboard, or controller, connected to
your computer is highly desirable at this stage.

1. Create a new blank Pro Tools session and name/save it.

2. Add one new mono Instrument Track (Command + Shift + N or
Control + Shift + N) (see **Fig. 69**).

Fig. 69

Notice the third setting in the dialog box (see **Fig. 70**)—there are five choices of track types in Pro Tools. Some of the other kinds of tracks will be mentioned a little later.

Fig. 70

3. Your new track will appear in orange on the far left of the Edit window. Change to Grid mode (in the top left-hand corner of your Edit window). This is probably wise to do whenever you start recording with MIDI data, especially if you wish to play roughly in time with a click track/metronome, and if you want to edit your data with precision.

4. Be aware of the tempo of your new session in Pro Tools. Look at the rulers at the top of the Edit window. Locate the one that says Tempo (or turn on the ruler from the View>Rulers menu). Look at the start of the ruler. You should see this (see **Fig. 71**).

Fig. 71

5. Assuming that your song is right at the beginning of the session (the main transport window reads 0:00:000), click on the little + button next to the word Tempo. The Tempo Change dialog appears (see **Fig. 72**).

Fig. 72

6. This is how you alter the tempo of your song. It's set to 120 beats per minute at present, but—this is very significant—you can always alter the tempo, *even after you have recorded your MIDI data* on the Instrument track. You can also always insert a tempo change in your song at any point—choose a point in your timeline, then follow the same steps as above.

7. You might also want the main transport controls in Pro Tools to be expressing everything in bars/beats. Go to that window and use the down arrow to change that setting (see **Fig. 73**).

Fig. 73

8. Now you should create a click track in your song so you have some kind of metronome to work with when you record (this is also useful when you record audio). To do this, go to Track>Create Click Track. Pro Tools creates a very narrow new track in your session, which should be green (see **Fig. 74**).

Fig. 74

9. Notice the S and M (Solo and Mute) buttons right next to the track name. You may not always want to hear the click track, so you can mute it if you need to. You're now ready to choose the sounds you need.

Using Virtual Instruments Inside Pro Tools— Xpand2! and Structure

You may wish to watch tutorial movie #21 on this topic.

Instrument tracks require you to "wire" a virtual instrument to them before you can choose the sounds you need, unlike simply creating a MIDI track with patches on your MIDI keyboard.

1. Open the Mix window, and go to the **Insert** area of the (orange) track (see **Fig. 75**).

2. Click on the first slot you see and choose Plug-in > Instrument > Xpand2 (mono). The Xpand2 plug-in window will appear (see **Fig. 76**).

Fig. 75

Notice the long list of other virtual instruments. There isn't time to explore all of them, but Xpand2 is perhaps the most useful to play with initially. They all work generally the same way.

Fig. 76

3. You now need to ensure that playing your keyboard will trigger Xpand's sounds. Try holding down some keys on your MIDI keyboard—you should now hear the "Beneath the Waves" sound that Xpand2 chooses by default. If you do not hear sound at this point, you may need to check your MIDI keyboard connections, and then return to this screen.

4. To select sounds in Xpand2, click on the tiny down arrow on the right-hand side of the instrument name "Beneath the Waves" (see **Fig. 77**).

5. Many different sounds will appear, organized into families. Experiment to find what you want. At this point, you're choosing which sound you want

Fig. 77

in slot A of Xpand2. If you wish, you can go to slots B, C, and D and start layering more sounds to go with the one you chose for slot A. The Level sliders control the overall mix you want to hear. There are many other settings inside the Xpand2 screen, including an arpeggiator and effects. Refer to the more complete Xpand2 tutorials and guides for more information—it is a very powerful synthesizer.

6. When you have dialed up the sounds you want, you can close the Xpand2 window—Pro Tools will remember your sounds. You can always click on the slot where Xpand2 is inserted to go back later and change sounds (see **Fig. 78**).

Fig. 78

7. **Record-enable** the Instrument track (the red circle in the track box on the left-hand side next to the orange bar), and make sure you're not using loop playback (Options>Loop Playback should not be checked). Press the Record button on the floating transport window, then press Play (or the spacebar) to begin recording. You should hear the click track playing. Play some notes on your MIDI keyboard. Press the spacebar or Stop. MIDI data should have been recorded, which you'll see. If you don't see data, check the settings described earlier.

8. To **hear** your MIDI performance, first ensure that your main cursor is set to the Smart tool, rewind to the beginning of your song (using the icon on the main transport window that looks like this) (see **Fig. 79**).

Fig. 79

9. Then press Play.

Don't forget that because you're not dealing with audio, you can continue to change sounds by going back to the Xpand2 instrument in the Mix window *after* you've recorded your MIDI notes, since it's just data at this point, not soundwaves.

If you need more Xpand2 sounds in your song, you'll need to create extra Instrument tracks and follow the same steps explained above, choosing different sounds—or experiment by inserting a different virtual instrument.

If you would like more drum choices, try playing around with **BFD Lite or** Structure Free in Pro Tools. Structure is a fantastic software instrument for creating groove tracks, and you can create separate instrument tracks for that instead of Xpand. There are great tutorial videos that come on the BFD disc showing you how to make the most of BFD Lite. Or you may prefer to use audio drum loops for all your rhythmic backing tracks—these are discussed in the next section of this guide.

Editing MIDI Data

One other piece of advice for this part: when editing MIDI you will most likely want to have Grid mode selected if it isn't already (you can change the mode in the top left of the Pro Tools Edit window), since you might want the data to "snap" to a more accurate place later in the song, rather than a random place, which will happen with Slip turned on.

When you have finished recording, always take your track out of record-enable (this will stop the red light flashing). Your MIDI data will probably look a bit like this when you have finished recording (see **Fig. 80**).

It's important to remember how to zoom in horizontally and vertically on the region at this stage (discussed earlier under zooming). A reminder: with the Smart tool selected, first click on the region you just recorded. Then press Command + [or] (Mac) or

Fig. 80

Control + [or] (Windows) to zoom horizontally, and press Control + the up/down arrows (Mac) or Start + the up/down arrows (Windows) to zoom vertically. Your MIDI data then might look like this (see **Fig. 81**).

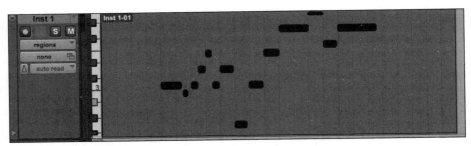

Fig. 81

It's so much easier to edit data if it is larger. Edit your data the same way as explained above with MIDI or audio data.

A couple of important things are different, though, when dealing with MIDI information. Look on the left-hand side of the Edit window, where the track name and color is. You'll see the word Regions. If you click on this, you'll immediately see other ways of viewing your data (see **Fig. 82**).

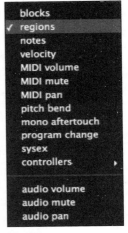

Fig. 82

Some of these are significant, like Notes and Velocity. If you switch the view to Notes, you can then click on individual notes and move them (again, with the Smart tool *always* enabled) (see **Fig. 83**).

A tiny finger appears to allow you to do that. If you change the view to Velocity, Pro Tools displays how hard you pressed the keys down when you played. These points can also be edited with your mouse by clicking and dragging (see **Fig. 84**).

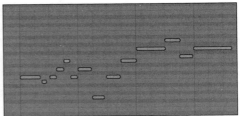

Fig. 83

Always return to viewing your MIDI data as a region after making changes in Notes and Velocity. Make sure you still have your MIDI data selected, or else Pro Tools won't know which data you want to edit from this point on.

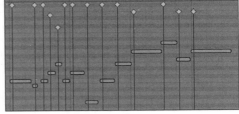

Fig. 84

Quantizing (cleaning up inaccuracies) is an important feature of MIDI recording. You can do it before or after you record. Go to Event>Event Operations>Quantize to see the settings you can change (see **Fig. 85**).

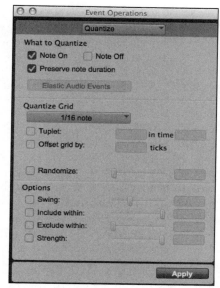

Learn the shortcut to open this window: Option/Alt + 0 (that's the zero above the O key on your main QWERTY keyboard).

It's very common to quantize MIDI data after you've played it, especially if you want it to sound in time with your click track on playback. Experiment with choosing a quantize value, click Apply, then undo this action, and try a different quantize until it sounds right.

Fig. 80

You'll see your MIDI data (or events) move slightly when you quantize them.

If you'd like to quantize *as you record* into Pro Tools (not afterward), go to Event>Event Operations>Input Quantize to set this up. Check the box that says *Enable Input Quantize*.

Cutting and Pasting MIDI Data

This is done almost exactly the same as with audio, discussed earlier. Always have the Smart tool enabled, and choose Regions as your method of displaying MIDI data (on the left-hand side of the Edit window, near the orange bar).

If you have Grid mode turned on, even better. The bars and beats of your song will be displayed as a light grid, and you can cut your data exactly on a barline or beat. Use the standard shortcut Command + E (Mac) or Control + E (Windows) to make a cut in your MIDI region (or select a section first by clicking and dragging, then use this shortcut). Any regions you don't want can be selected and deleted with the Delete or backspace key. You can drag the MIDI data to the left or right. Notice the data appears to *snap* to the nearest bar or beat when you do this in Grid mode. Remember how to alter your grid settings at the top of the main Edit window.

1. To repeat your MIDI events, select the region first, and type Option + Alt + R to open up the Repeat dialog box (see **Fig. 86**).

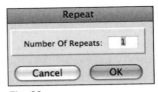

Fig. 86

2. Choose how many repeats you want, and click OK.

Other Views of MIDI Data

You can view MIDI data in various other ways too, which may be useful from time to time. These options can all be found in the Window menu. Select the region you would like to view first.

MIDI Editor

First, go to Window>MIDI editor (Control + = or Start + =). This is a nice large dialog box that allows you to move notes up and down, with a clear piano display on the left-hand side. You can play back your MIDI with this window open, as well as edit the data. Close this window manually when you have finished editing the data (see **Fig. 87**).

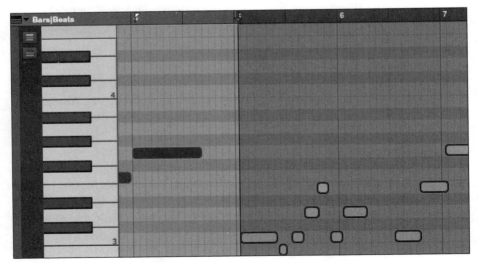

Fig. 87

Score Editor

To open this, go to Window>Score Editor (Control + Option + = or Start + Alt + =). This is a notation display with lots of options (it's a mini version of the software program Sibelius). Note the tools in the top left-hand corner of this window (see **Fig. 88**).

You can play back your MIDI with this window open, as well as edit the data. You can also print out your MIDI data with this dialog open. Consult your Pro Tools Reference Guide for further details.

Fig. 88

MIDI Event List

The final data view can be seen by going to Window > MIDI Event List (Option/ Alt + =). This is perhaps the least friendly view, but some people like to work with this window—in fact, most MIDI sequencers used to only have this view for many years!

As before, you can play back your MIDI with this window open, as well edit the data (see **Fig. 89**).

You can actually open several MIDI event windows simultaneously if you wish, and if there's a particular window that you commonly use,

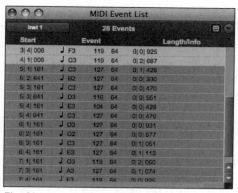

Fig. 89

you can set that up in the Preferences settings for Pro Tools, so when you double-click on a MIDI region it will open up the editing window you prefer.

Go to the Preferences screen of Pro Tools (in the Pro Tools menu on the top left for Mac, or the File menu for Windows). Go to the tab that says MIDI, and note this part of that page (see **Fig. 90**).

Fig. 90

One Final MIDI View

If you look in the main Pro Tools Edit window at the orange bar for your Instrument track on the far left, you'll notice an arrow at the bottom of it: Click on this arrow, and it will most likely display velocity (see **Fig. 91**).

There are choices there, too. Click on the down arrow next to the word Velocity, and you will see more potential views. Think of that screen as a secondary or dual view of your MIDI data.

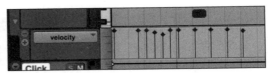

Fig. 91

For multitrack MIDI recording, keep adding more Instrument (or MIDI) tracks, and follow the same steps as above. As a general rule, try and avoid using more than 16 tracks of MIDI, since your sound playback source may get confused. There are officially only 16 MIDI channels—each track should use a different channel! Drums are reserved for channel 10 in a standard MIDI setup.

Also, if you create multiple Instrument tracks, and insert Xpand2 multiple times, bear in mind that this will eventually put a strain on your computer processor. You will eventually wish to *render* your Instrument tracks as MIDI data (watch tutorial movie #26 for more information on how to do this).

Using Loops and Recording/Editing New Audio

Accompanying this section of the Teach Yourself Guide, you should watch tutorial movies #28–31 and also movies #15, 18, and 40 on the accompanying DVD—these follow the same steps that are being covered.

Loops and the Workspace Window—Auditioning and Importing

Pro Tools comes with a huge amount of predefined musical material, called audio loops. These are precut into snippets usually a measure or two long, and their tempo is given in the name of the file. Ensure that you have installed all of these loops—be warned, they take up quite a lot of disk space, because there are so many of them!

These loops are often the perfect building blocks for a songwriter, particularly if you are working without a drummer and you haven't got time to set up and record a drum kit or record your own drum tracks using MIDI or Instrument tracks.

1. Start a new blank Pro Tools session (and turn on Grid mode, which is important when dealing with time-sensitive material like drum loops).

2. You can import drum loops the same way as any other audio, but you have some more flexibility if you bring them in via the workspace window. Watch tutorial movie #15 on this topic. In essence, you can audition your drum loop at the speed of your Pro Tools session, which may not necessarily be the same speed as the drum loop. You can either bring the loop in at its original tempo *or* at the tempo of your current Pro Tools session. Either way, if you're working with time-sensitive material like a drum loop, it's good practice to match the tempo of your Pro Tools session to that of your loops, or vice-versa.

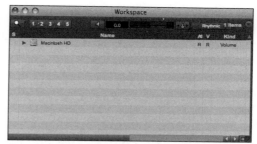

Fig. 92

3. To access the Workspace window, go to Window> Workspace or use the shortcut Option/Alt ; (semi-colon). It will initially look like this (see **Fig. 92**).

You can resize the workspace window.

Fig. 93

4. Click on the hard-drive icon to drill down and find where your drum loops are (assuming they are on an accessible hard drive). When you have located them, they will appear like this (see **Fig. 93**).

5. Click again and Pro Tools will display all the loops and give you a speaker icon that allows you to audition each loop to see if you want to use it (see **Fig. 94**).

6. At this point, be aware of the tempo of your Pro Tools session behind the workspace window. If you didn't choose a tempo, your Pro Tools session will be at 120 bpm (beats per

Fig. 94

minute). If you have auditioned a drum loop from Pro Tools' Big Fish collection, it will most likely include the tempo of the loop in the name (i.e., 129 16th Rock Drum Verse 03.wav: the loop is at 129 bpm).

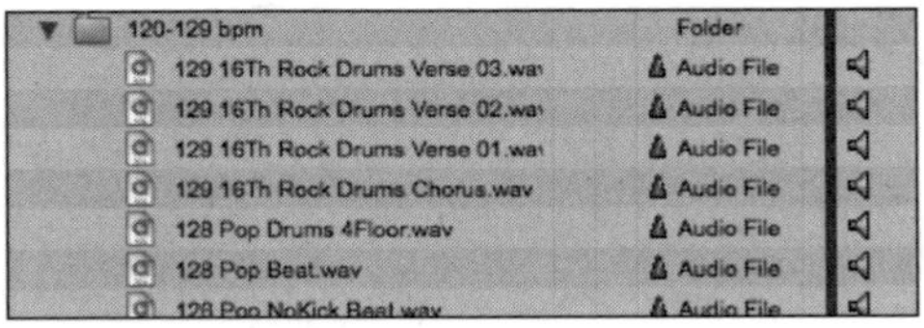

7. Now look at the top of your workspace window, and you'll see a metronome icon like this (see **Fig. 95**).

Fig. 95

8. Highlight that metronome icon (it will turn green) and audition your loop once again—now your loop will play at the speed of your Pro Tools session, which may be either slower or faster. You can immediately tell whether the loop will work. At this point you may want to alter the Pro Tools session's tempo to match your loop, or you might want to import the loop at the tempo of your Pro Tools session. Having this flexibility is great.

9. You can drag and drop the loop straight from your workspace window onto the Edit window of your song with the mouse. If you do this, Pro Tools may give you this warning message (see **Fig. 96**).

Fig. 96

10. If you choose to Import the tempo from the loop, it will automatically change the tempo of your Pro Tools session to match the original tempo of your drum loop. If you choose *not* to import the tempo from the file, Pro Tools will retain your session's original tempo (in this case, 120 bpm), and it will make the drum loop conform to the tempo of your session (effectively applying the TCE tool automatically, and stretching or contracting your audio automatically). This is a huge time-saver.

11. Don't forget to zoom in horizontally on your loop to take a closer look. You can also repeat the loop using the skills learned earlier in this guide.

Getting Ready to Record Live in Pro Tools

After importing loops into your song, you can quickly create a rhythmic backing track, which is perfect for songwriters. Let's assume that you want to record your voice with a microphone, or play an electric guitar into Pro Tools.

1. Create a new track in Pro Tools, using the usual shortcut Command + Shift + N (Mac) or Control + Shift + N (Windows).

2. Choose one mono audio track from the dialog box. Your new track will appear.

Setting Proper Levels

When recording into Pro Tools, it's essential to set your input levels correctly. When you record into Pro Tools, your signal is converted from an analog waveform to digital bits. While Pro Tools provides you with faders to control the level inside the computer, this only works if you bring the proper level into Pro Tools. This is done on the physical interface itself and not in the software.

When you record-enable a track, Pro Tools will allow you to visually monitor the incoming signal, which you'll need to watch as you work. However, you need to adjust the physical input knobs on your hardware. It's easy to remember: When recording, tweak the knobs on your audio interface. When mixing, tweak the software controls!

Digital signal theory is very simple: You mustn't go into the red. Each meter reads back the incoming signal on a scale where 0 dB is the loudest signal and –96 dB is the softest. You simply shouldn't exceed 0 dB on input. This is easy to avoid and impossible to fix after the fact.

Fig. 97

1. Plug in your guitar or position your microphone and enable record mode in your track by clicking on the red circle near the track name (see **Fig. 97**).

2. Watch the input meter (you can see this in the Edit window or the Mix window), and play what you feel is the loudest part in your piece. The meter will hit red if the level is too high; the bottom of the strip also gives you a numerical readout. You should aim for a level of about –6 dB when you record.

   Remember, you can raise the level to your heart's content later in the software, but if you exceed 0 dB on input, you will "clip" the waveform and ruin the recording. There is literally nothing you can do to fix a poorly recorded performance. Recording a clean signal into Pro Tools ensures that you'll be able to add effects and mix down to a final, polished, professional recording.

3. You may need to do some troubleshooting if you can't seem to get any signal from your microphone or guitar. Remember which input you're using on your audio interface (if you have an interface with more than one input). Go to the Mix window and check that you've set the correct input there (where it says I/O) (see **Fig. 98**).

Fig. 98

4. If you're using a microphone, there are two vital things to remember: 1) always turn the speakers off and use headphones (or you'll encounter feedback); and 2) if it's a condenser microphone, you'll need to activate the *phantom power* or 48V button on your audio interface.

Recording

As you've been testing the input signal, you should have been able to hear yourself, or to "monitor" the incoming signal. You're actually hearing *two* signals—the signal you're sending to Pro Tools, and the signal you're hearing back from Pro Tools. If there's a significant delay between the two and you find this annoying, you can mute your track in the Mix or Edit window so you only hear the signal being sent. Click on the M button to mute your signal (see **Fig. 99**).

Fig. 99

Pressing Mute while you record won't prevent your track from being recorded! ***Note:*** *current Mbox3 interfaces for Pro Tools now allow onboard low-latency monitoring, so there is no need to mute the track on which you are recording–you should only experience a small delay between the two signals (incoming and outgoing).*

1. If you're using extra hardware for your guitar, like your own effects box, plug the guitar into that first, and from there into the Pro Tools hardware. Also remember that you can add effects later. *If you're a guitarist, you may wish to investigate an alternative audio interface, the Eleven Rack, designed for Pro Tools LE. It has a huge range of extremely useful sounds and is designed to work seamlessly while you record into Pro Tools.*

2. Some people like to record their vocals/audio with reverb to improve their performance. To do this you can set up an aux input and send the vocal signal to a reverb plug-in (see the section in this guide on using audio plug-ins for how to add reverb to a mix), but the great thing

is that you won't be recording the reverb: it'll only be present in your headphones: you can add it later on in the final mix if you want. Try not to add too many extras into the loop when you're recording, though, as it slows down the computer.

3. Once you're satisfied with everything, and you can hear a decent mix between the backing track(s) already recorded and what you're about to record, record-enable your track (hit the Record button on the main transport window), ensure that you're at the correct point in the song, and press Play. This will initiate recording.

4. Press the spacebar to stop recording.

Using Different Takes (Track Comping)

You may wish to view tutorial movie #31 on this topic.

A powerful feature in Pro Tools is the ability to record multiple "takes" or "performances" within the same track. This is useful for recording a difficult section multiple times and picking the best parts from each recording.

1. To activate this feature, go to Pro Tools>Preferences (Mac) or File> Preferences (Windows) and go to the tab that says Operation. Check the box on the right-hand side that says "Automatically Create New Playlists When Loop Recording" (see **Fig. 100**).

 Automatically Create New Playlists When Loop Recording

Fig. 100

Now Pro Tools will save each version or take of your track as you record, and you can review them later.

Loop Recording

2. Next, activate Loop Recording in Pro Tools, so that Pro Tools will continually loop around a section of your song while you record. The shortcut to activate this is Option/ Alt + L (or go to Option>Loop Record). When you do this, you'll notice that the Record icon in the main transport window or in the playback controls at the top of your Pro Tools Edit window now looks like this (see **Fig. 101**).

Fig. 101

3. Then, select the section of your song over which you wish to do the recording. Here is the best way to do this: Go to the main time display window at the top of the Edit screen, and ensure that you are displaying your song in Bars/Beats rather than absolute time (see **Fig. 102**).

Fig. 102

4. Now look at the numbers next to the word Start and End (see **Fig. 103**).

Fig. 103

5. If the location is incorrect, click on the number that needs to change, and type in the bar numbers around which you wish to loop (hit Enter or Return after you are done typing, so Pro Tools stores the numbers). It will look something like this when you are done (see **Fig. 104**).

Fig. 104

6. Incidentally, another way of selecting a section to record over, if you are working with existing backing tracks that are already in your session rather than a totally blank session, is to select an existing region of audio in another track with your mouse, like this (see **Fig. 105**).

Fig. 105

Don't worry—even though you have selected an audio region on another track, it won't be recorded over, because you *won't* be record-enabling that track—obviously you will just record-enable the track you do wish to record into.

Notice in the figure above that the Start and End numbers in the floating transport window have also reflected your selection—so you may find this an easier way of selecting your record area.

Using Pre-roll

7. Lastly, you may wish to activate a very useful feature called *pre-roll*. This allows Pro Tools to play or count-in for a given number of measures *before* it starts recording—it's really annoying if you start recording by clicking on the mouse, and have no time to grab your instrument and start playing! To turn this on, go to the floating transport window, click on the word Pre-roll, and choose how many measures you need (for example, 2). It should look like this (see **Fig. 106**).

Fig. 106

   Watch out—Pro Tools remembers that pre-roll setting until you deactivate that button—it will pre-roll every time you play or record.

8. Now start recording, and Pro Tools will automatically loop around your section, and begin creating extra takes each time—it won't overdub, or wipe what you previously recorded.

9. Once you are finished (perhaps you made several passes through the same section, and played some bits well in different passes), you can view the different takes, or combine them into one finished take (where you assemble the best bits of what you played).

10. First, take the track out of record-enable mode, and zoom in horizontally if you need to. To view the different takes you played (you may have seen them being displayed as you were recording), note the little down arrow just to the right of your track name (in the Edit window) (see **Fig. 107**).

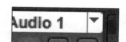

Fig. 107

11. Click on this arrow and you'll see that the different takes you recorded are listed and numbered (see **Fig. 108**).

12. You can click on each take and listen to it. If you're totally happy with one of the takes, just use that one, but if you need to assemble a composite take (that is, gather the best parts from each of your takes), create a new audio track, select the bits you liked from

Fig. 108

each take (taking great care not to drag them out of time), cut them into separate mini regions, and drag them down onto your new track like so (see **Fig. 109**).

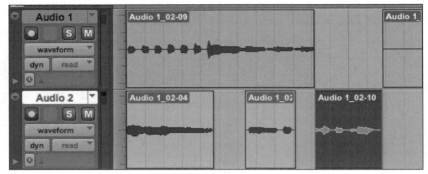

Fig. 109

13. You can then mute or delete the old track, or select and join together all of your takes (assembled on the new track as mini regions) into one consolidated region, using the shortcut we learned earlier: Option + Shift + 3 (Mac) or Alt + Shift + 3 (Windows) (see **Figs. 110A** and **110B**).

Fig. 110a

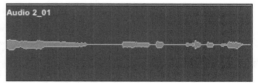

Fig. 110b

Punch or Overdub Recording

The ability to drop in and rerecord over part of an existing recording is a critical skill. Often when recording, you'll find you only want to redo a small part, without recording the whole track again.

You can of course use the technique employed above (recording multiple takes or track compositing), or you can create a whole new track and simply mute your previous track, later joining together the bits you liked by selecting them, cutting the audio into smaller regions, and dragging your best bits all into one final track, but you can also simply drop in and record over part of an existing track.

1. *Turn off* loop recording (Option/Alt + L).

2. Employ the techniques discussed above, using Pre-roll to give yourself a few measures of count-in before Pro Tools starts recording.

3. Select just the part of the song you need to record over (click and drag over the region you need to work on—Grid mode is very useful for making precise selections).

4. Record-enable your track, check your levels, and start recording. Don't panic—Pro Tools will *only* record over the section you have selected, and if you use Pre-roll, you'll hear the track playing beforehand, so you can play along until the section you want to rerecord comes up. Some people (vocalists especially) like to have many measures of pre-roll set up so they can get the groove of the song well in advance, and can sing along with the track until Pro Tools drops them in for recording, and drops them out automatically at the end.

Other Recording Advice

Here's an important consideration: *Make sure you have enough hard drive space on your computer before you start a project!* A separate, large hard drive to "archive" your projects is an essential purchase. Pro Tools prefers that you record onto an external USB or FireWire hard drive instead of your local hard drive.

Most songs are done from the "ground up"; that is, the basic rhythmic tracks are created first, then the melodic and harmonic content is added. A click track is critical to help you stay in time, as is Grid mode and working with bars/beats, unless you are recording music with no fixed time at all.

Create as many audio tracks as you need. There's also nothing wrong with creating "guide" or scratch tracks that won't be used later, such as an ultra-simple chord progression with a basic rhythm to help "guide" other musicians through the song.

Once a track is recorded, you can turn off the input entirely, and just leave the output. Audio tracks will be in blue in the Mix window. MIDI tracks will be purple. Instrument tracks will be orange. If you created a click track, that will also have its own fader, in green.

Don't forget to use **markers** in your song to help you find your way around! These were discussed earlier in this guide.

Using Strip Silence for Voiceover and Podcasting Tracks

See tutorial movie #40 for this topic.

An excellent audio processing tool for when you record a voiceover track, Strip Silence lets you quickly locate points in your vocal recording where there is background noise, coughs, or breathing, allowing all of these things to be isolated and then removed.

1. Take a look at this region of a voiceover recording (or perhaps find your own region from your own recordings) (see **Fig. 111**).

   The loud transient at the start is probably a cough. You can then see the audio waveform with gaps in between— these might contain room noise, breathing, background talking, etc.

   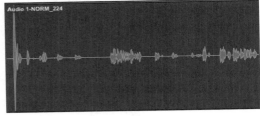
   Fig. 111

2. If you select the whole region and type Command + U (Mac) or Control + U (Windows) to activate the Strip Silence plug-in, you will see something like the following (see **Fig. 112**).

   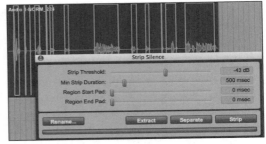
   Fig. 112

3. The plug-in window has appeared, and the audio has been divided up. Pro Tools is searching for the parts of the region that are above a certain noise level. Look at the slider that says Strip Threshold and drag it from left to right with your mouse. Think of this as the *sensitivity*. It is measured in decibels (dB) on the right-hand side.

4. As you drag the slider to the left, you are lowering the threshold, and more audio will be "saved." As you move it to the right, Pro Tools will only look for the audio above the decibel level indicated, and will then remove all the audio that falls below that level (i.e., the quieter bits). Setting the slider at around –43 dB is an optimal position, although this

will vary depending on how loud the audio is in the first place.

5. Please don't neglect to use the excellent Normalize plug-in to make your audio louder—discussed earlier under "Editing Existing Audio."

6. When you have the settings the way you would like, click the Strip button, and the lower-volume audio will disappear. Close the Strip Silence floating window, and your region will look something like this (see **Fig. 113**).

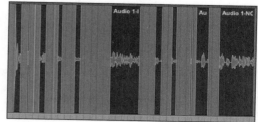

Fig. 113

7. Zoom in horizontally on the audio (as always) and check that it plays back okay. If there are bits that were missed, hit Undo and re-run the plug-in with a different threshold setting. If a few bits of unwanted noise are still present, you can now select and delete them individually, since the plug-in has effectively chopped the audio up into lots of small regions.

8. Lastly, *consolidate* all the small regions together, using the same shortcut discussed earlier. Select all the regions by Shift-clicking them, then type the shortcut Shift + Option + 3 (Mac) or Shift + Alt + 3 (Windows). You are done!

If you do a lot of voice work, this plug-in (as well as the Normalize plug-in) is absolutely indispensable.

Using Elastic Time/Elastic Audio in Pro Tools

Tutorial movie #18 walks you through this sophisticated feature in Pro Tools.

As we discussed earlier on in this guide, the TCE (Time Compression/Expansion) tool is a way of easily stretching or squeezing existing audio so that it lasts for a different length of time, *without* altering the pitch. We also discussed pitch shifting using the AudioSuite plug-in.

Elastic Time (sometimes referred to as Elastic Audio) is somewhat different, and is a more recent feature in Pro Tools. With Elastic Time, Pro Tools detects where the louder points are (known as *transients*) in an audio region or audio loop, allowing you to shift these individual transients around within the audio.

So this feature lets you treat audio the same way as MIDI—for example, you can now *quantize* or auto-correct the timing of audio without having to rerecord it, or make other advanced changes inside your audio in a manual way. It is especially useful for rhythmic, repetitious material, like a drum track or rhythm guitar track. The tutorial movie focuses on fixing a guitar performance. Let's review the steps required to do this, using Elastic Time/Elastic Audio.

1. First, let's find some audio to work on. You can either start a new session in Pro Tools and record your own rhythmical playing or drum loop, or use what is provided with these materials. For example, a Pro Tools session is included in Module One of this guide, called "Module One Jam." Open this and you'll see a session with five different tracks in it. Mute all the tracks except for the last one, called Rhythm Guitar. Play it to hear the performance.

2. Add a click track into the session (Track>Create Click track) and listen again to the timing on playback. It isn't in time! This is because the song should be at a tempo of 102 bpm, not 120 bpm, as it currently is.

3. Change the tempo of the song by first making sure you have rewound to the beginning using the return to zero button.

Fig. 18b

4. Then look at the Tempo ruler and the plus sign next to the word tempo.

Click on the button to get the tempo change dialog, and type 102 followed by OK. Now listen to the song again, with the click track. The guitar is closer to the beat. Having the correct tempo is critical when you use Elastic Time, as next we will quantize the guitar playing (or auto-correct its timing) to 102 beats per minute.

Fig. 17

5. Zoom in horizontally on the selected audio to make it appear wider—this is important for what is about to happen. The usual shortcut applies: Command + [or] (Mac) or Control + [or] (Windows).

6. Also zoom in vertically on the track—use the shortcut mentioned earlier in the guide; or you can do this manually, as in the tutorial movie—click on the down arrow that you see on the far left, on the track bar, right next to the track name (see **Fig. 114**).

You'll see several choices (see **Fig. 115**).

Choose Jumbo as the track height. Scroll down the session to ensure you can see all of the guitar track region.

Fig. 114

7. Look again near where the track name is, and locate the tiny blue icon below where it says the track name and the word waveform (see **Fig. 116**).

Click on that icon, and it brings up two choices: Samples or Ticks. It is set to samples at present (the default Pro Tools setting for audio). Change it to Ticks (a tiny green metronome will appear instead, a little like what we saw earlier in the Workspace window). Without getting too technical, making that change means that this particular audio (the guitar performance) can now have its timing transformed—not something you would normally want to have happen most of the time. It is now *tick based* rather than *sample based*.

Fig. 115

Fig. 116

8. Click on the gray icon right next to what is now the green metronome. This box appears (see **Fig. 117**).

You'll see that the default setting is *Disable Elastic Audio*. Change this setting to the word *Rhythmic*. You are effectively telling Pro Tools what style of playing the audio is, so the Elastic Time function knows what to do. At this point, Pro Tools goes to work in the background and analyzes what is going on in the region.

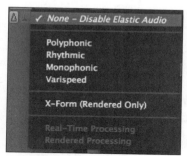

Fig. 117

9. Let's see what Pro Tools has done. Again look at the far left of the track, where the track name is, and click on the word *Waveform*. The following choices appear (see **Fig. 118**).

10. We looked at this box earlier in the guide when we viewed the volume level of a track. This time,

Fig. 118

choose *Analysis,* and see what Pro Tools now displays in your region (see **Fig. 119**).

Fig. 119

In essence, it shows lots and lots of tiny lines, which mark the transient points in the audio (the strong beats). Try zooming in even more horizontally to see more detail (see **Fig. 120**).

Compare these transients to the bars/beats timeline at the top of the screen, and think about it. If the playing was perfectly rhythmical, every note would line up exactly to a sixteenth note or eighth note in the timeline bars/beats ruler. There may be a few inaccuracies.

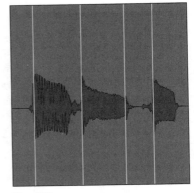

Fig. 120

11. Now comes the magic part. We are going to try and quantize these transient lines to make them line up slightly more accurately. (This is where audio behaves exactly like the MIDI data that we covered earlier in this guide.) Make sure the region is still selected (it should be) and open the Quantize dialog box (Option/Alt + 0—that's the zero above the P key on your QWERTY keyboard) (see **Fig. 121**).

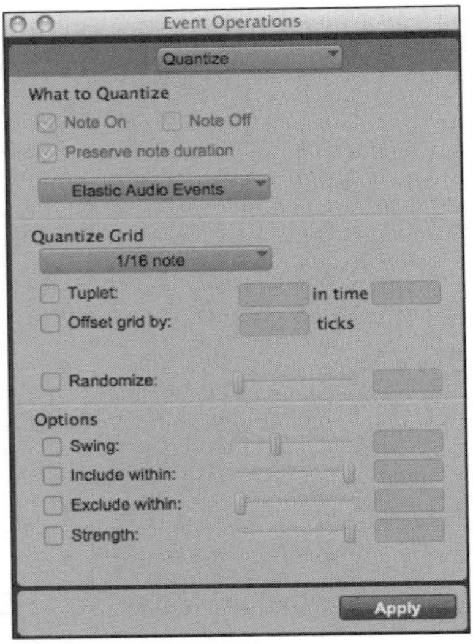

12. Notice that the words Elastic Audio Events are lit in this dialog—Pro Tools is guessing that you are going to want to quantize those events and nothing else. Notice the quantize grid says 1/16 note (16th notes). It is going to "round up" these Elastic Audio events to

Fig. 121

the nearest 16th pulse. Click Apply and watch the lines move slightly. You can always undo and redo to see the effect, if you missed it! (Hit Command + Z or Control + Z to undo your last action, and Command + Y or Control + Y to redo that action.)

13. Have a listen to the change that has happened. Close the quantize dialog box and play back the audio. It may still need a few more fixes, and you can also manually adjust where the transients are, but that is getting into advanced territory—consult the Pro Tools Reference Guide. Finish by changing the audio view from analysis back to waveform on the far left.

Elastic analysis and processing of audio is one of the Holy Grail features of an audio program. Try experimenting with this feature yourself. It works best on fixing rhythmical playing; it is much harder for it to analyze and fix a single melody, for example. For those cases, it can be best to go back to the old-fashioned way of zooming in, selecting a tiny portion of audio, creating a region just for that, and nudging it left and right (see the section on nudging earlier in this guide).

Multitrack Sessions and Learning to Mix/Master

See tutorial movies #32–35 on the accompanying DVD—these follow the same steps that are being covered.

There are several multitrack sessions provided with this guide, intended for use in Module Five of the curriculum. In following along with this section, you may wish to open up and use one of them.

What Is a Multitrack Session?

In many respects, editing a Pro Tools session with lots of tracks in it (known as a *multitrack* session) is no different from working with a single track of audio, as discussed earlier. All the basic steps of selecting and editing audio are identical. The same is true of a session that has multiple tracks of MIDI in it. This section, though, is more about learning how to mix, and any extra steps one needs to be mindful of when dealing with lots of tracks.

The most basic aspect of mixing is balance. We control the audio balance in two ways: 1) front to back through volume changes; and 2) right-to-left through track panning (when a track is a *mono* and not a *stereo* track). To bring an instrument into focus, use the fader in the Mix window to balance its sound against the other tracks. This brings instruments into the foreground when needed and others into the background. Right to left panning is also very important.

Panning

Think of an acoustic ensemble: Each instrument in that ensemble sits in its own distinct place on the stage when they perform live. Most likely, each instrument will be recorded with a single microphone, and will be recorded as a *mono* track in your session. By default, all new mono tracks in Pro Tools are panned dead center. You'll want to adjust this panning to the right or left to create the illusion of a "sound stage" in your recording when it plays back through stereo (left and right) speakers. Proper volume and pan changes can begin to refine a mix.

Fig. 122

1. Open up a session in Pro Tools that has mono audio tracks in it, and go to the Mix window. The shortcut, as always, is Command + = (Mac) or Control + = (Windows).

2. You can adjust the panning of any track by looking above the track's fader, where there is a panning knob (see **Fig. 122**).

3. Use your mouse (click and drag up or down) to adjust the panning from left to right. You'll see a numerical readout of how much you have panned the track in the stereo spectrum.

Adding Effects to Your Mix

Next, you'll want some effects.

Before you start to mix your song, it's worth understanding how you can add effects to dramatically enhance the sound. You need to think about something called the *signal path*, because you have several choices about *when* and *where* to add effects like reverb, EQ, compression, and delay/echo. You may need to deal with several tracks at once, and your computer may run out of gas if you wire things up incorrectly.

There are several different kinds of **effects**, the most common being those discussed earlier in this guide, including EQ (equalization—boosting or cutting the frequencies of each audio track), reverb (sometimes referred to as *echo* or *reverberation*, simulating real acoustic spaces), and compression/limiting (adjusting the dynamic range of a signal to lessen or enhance the difference between loud and soft sections).

For more information about what each of these effects does, refer to resources such as *The Everything Guide to Digital Home Recording* (talked about in the curriculum part of this book).

Insert Effects

Compression and EQ should be added as an *insert* effects, as we learned earlier in this guide in the section on editing existing audio. This is because if you add EQ or compression to a track, it should be added to the whole track, and only that track. You wouldn't want to *partially* add EQ or compression to a track. It either has EQ or it doesn't. You can make the EQ or compression very subtle, and you can bypass it, but you definitely *insert* the effect into a track, right at the beginning of the signal chain.

At this point you should definitely work on adding EQ and compression to various tracks in your session. Don't forget to use the Solo button in the Mix or Edit window to solo a track, and then insert an EQ (follow the steps earlier in this guide) and see if you can make that track sound better.

Adding EQ is an imprecise art. Once a track sounds good, the next question is whether it works in the context of the song. Much practice is required to become adept at handling EQ (and compression). Some tracks may not need any EQ or compression at all.

Why Reverb and Delay Should Be Treated Differently

Reverb and delay/echo are different because you are simulating (in a computer) how real sound reverberates, so these effects should be added to the mix in a different way than compression/EQ. You do this by using *auxiliary inputs*, creating a *bus* and a *send/return* (more on this below). Think of these kinds of effects as being more like adding salt or pepper when cooking—they should be used somewhat sparingly.

In an ideal world, you would want to be able to compare each track *without* reverb to the same track *with* reverb, and you would want to be able to control the balance between them in a subtle way. That's where using an auxiliary input helps a great deal. Using an aux send also uses less computer memory, as you only have to load one instance of a reverb in your whole mix, and then *send* tracks to the reverb you have created.

You might want several or all the tracks in your song to be affected by the *same* reverb; you wouldn't do that with EQ, which is more unique to a particular track's needs.

Earlier in this guide, we did use reverb in the same way as EQ and compression (as an *insert* effect), and that is sometimes okay to do, but it isn't good practice when you work with multitrack sessions.

Now take a look at the two diagrams below.

Diagram A shows how you add *insert* effects (EQ, compression) to a track in a Pro Tools session. You control the *level* of these effects with a few mouse clicks.

Diagram B shows how you add effects like reverb and delay/echo to a track in a Pro Tools session, by *sending* part of the signal to an *auxiliary input* (or *aux input*). For this to work, you have to use an intermediate step, called *bussing*. A bus is simply a virtual cable that connects your channels together. More in a minute!

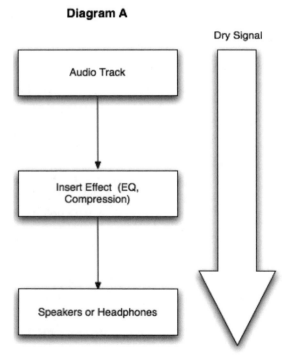

Diagram A

Diagram B

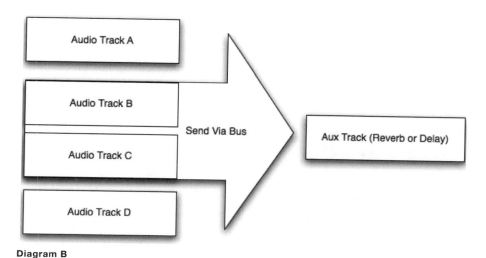

Diagram B

Adding Aux Send Effects to Recordings

1. First, open up one of the multitrack sessions included with this guide (designed for use in Module Five), or create your own recording.

2. Go to the Mix window, and you will see there are a lot of tracks. If all the tracks don't quite fit onto the screen, go to the main Pro Tools View menu and choose Narrow Mix—or learn the excellent shortcut Command + Option + M (Mac) or Control + Alt + M (Windows).

3. You might want to listen to a single track to start off with and mute all the other tracks, or else the following steps may become confusing, with too much going on musically to hear.

4. Make sure you can hear the soloed track clearly in the song. You may want to select a section of that track, in the Edit menu (see **Fig. 123**).

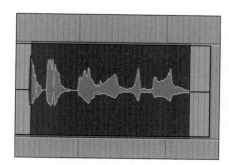

Fig. 123

Press the spacebar to play and make sure you're just hearing that track at that moment in the song. If a region is selected before you press Play, Pro Tools just plays that part of the song. If all the other tracks are muted, you'll only hear that part of the track.

5. Now turn on Loop Playback in Pro Tools (Command/Control + Shift + L). Notice that the Play icon in the transport window changes its appearance.

Creating an Aux Input Track and Adding Reverb

See tutorial movie #34.

6. We'll add reverb to this track first. Once you master this task, you can do the same for the other tracks, and gradually unmute them and listen to the effect. Type Command + Shift + N (Mac) or Control + Shift + N (Windows), and create one stereo Aux Input track (see **Fig. 124**).

Fig. 124

This will be used to control the reverb in your song. Rename the track if you like, such as *Reverb*. (You can rename any track in Pro Tools by double-clicking on where you see the track name in either the Edit or Mix windows.) Later, you may need to create a separate Aux Input track if you want to add a separate effect such as delay into your song. Use one aux input for each effect you need in a song.

7. If you look in the Mix window of the session, your audio track(s) will most likely be blue, and the new Aux Input track will be green (see **Fig. 125**).

Fig. 125

On the blue *audio track* that you'd like to work on, move the mouse to Send Selector A (this is toward the top of the channel strip, below the insert points), and select Bus>Bus 1-2 (Stereo) (see **Fig. 126**).

A new extra floating window will appear with a fader. This is called the *bus fader*. This fader will control how much signal from your audio track goes to the Aux Input track (see **Fig. 127**).

8. Now locate the *input* on the green Aux Input track. It's below the words I/O (see **Fig. 128**).

9. Click where it says *no input* and choose bus>Bus 1-2 (Stereo) (see **Fig. 129**).

   This provides the essential link between your audio track and your Aux Input track (as though you had physically wired them together). There's still no reverb yet! One more step.

Fig. 126

Fig. 127

10. Next, we add the desired effect to the green Aux Input track. Go to the Insert area (at the top of the aux input strip) and choose Multi-channel Plug-in>Reverb>D-Verb (Stereo) (see **Fig. 130**).

   You have now chosen the reverb to use in the song, and the reverb floating window *also* appears (we looked at this earlier in this guide). Reposition and resize things if you need to. You're ready to start experimenting with your song.

11. Start playing the track. To add reverb, you need to send signal from your audio track to your bus. This is done by adjusting the *bus fader* (that extra floating window), which is at zero by default.

Fig. 128

Fig. 129

12. Raise the fader with your mouse while the track plays. (A reminder: You should mute all the other tracks in your song. Perhaps set up loop playback over a selected region, as discussed earlier). How much reverb you send is up to your personal taste. You should now see signal appearing in the Aux Input track. The fader on the Aux Input track controls how much reverb is present in the mix. Raise and lower this to taste.

Fig. 130

In short, the floating bus fader track acts as a wet/dry mix (wet = lots or reverb; dry = nothing). The fader on the Aux Input acts as a reverb master fader.

13. If you are dealing with multiple audio tracks that all need reverb on them, remember that each track needs to be sent to the *same bus* if you wish to use the same reverb on each track (highly recommended and normal practice).

14. Finally, if you're wondering what the fader does that's on the green Aux Input track in the Mix window, that controls the overall amount of reverb that you have at your disposal (in this instance). It's probably best not to adjust this—leave that fader where it was when you first created the Aux Input track.

Wiring Up More Tracks to Your Aux Input

There's no need to create more Aux Input tracks. All you need to do is use the Send part of each audio track's channel strip to connect it to the existing Aux Input track you've already created. The Send area is in the Mix window here (use the first slot) (see **Fig. 131**).

Fig. 131

Each time you do this, you'll see the floating *bus fader* window changes to the one you just created. Instead of Pro Tools creating multiple floating windows, it just displays the last one you created or worked on. Listen and adjust the slider as before. If you need to return to check the level of your first track's bus fader, click on it in the channel strip (see **Fig. 132**).

Fig. 132

Incidentally, if you make adjustments to the *reverb settings* in the floating reverb window, they will obviously affect all the tracks that are being bussed to the aux input you created. Also, having different reverbs in the same song can sound very strange! It is more normal to choose one reverb that will be used by all tracks in your song.

Each track, though, can have a different amount of signal sent to the aux input, of course. So some tracks can end up with more reverb than others, but it's the *same* reverb. This is done via the bus fader for each track. If you'd like to check the effect on an individual track, simply solo it, using the S button on the individual audio track.

As you start to explore effects, you'll see lots of knobs and sliders. Don't fear ... play with the settings until you find something you like!

TIP   When adding reverb, if you can tell that the effect is present, you've added too much. It should not sound like Notre Dame Cathedral. Just add a little bit and flavor to taste.

If you also need to add delay/echo, create an extra aux input channel and repeat the same steps, but use different busses, such as 3-4, so you can send signals from your tracks to two separate effects using different busses.

Grouping Tracks Together

See tutorial movie #33.

In essence, grouping tracks together is useful for making multiple volume changes, or muting multiple tracks, at once. It can also be useful from a visual perspective. If you have a song with four or five guitar tracks, you can group all of these together so it's easier to work with them when doing a final mix.

1. First, open a multitrack session (there are several provided with this guide).

2. Then go to the Mix window and look at the white column on the left-hand side of the mixer that says Tracks & Groups. If it isn't being displayed, click on the small arrow you see right at the bottom left-hand corner of the Mix window to open this extra pane up (see **Fig. 133**).

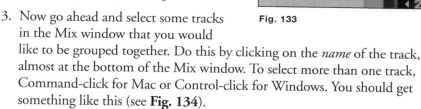

Fig. 133

3. Now go ahead and select some tracks in the Mix window that you would like to be grouped together. Do this by clicking on the *name* of the track, almost at the bottom of the Mix window. To select more than one track, Command-click for Mac or Control-click for Windows. You should get something like this (see **Fig. 134**).

4. Now type Command + G (Mac) or Control + G (Windows). The Groups dialog box appears (see **Fig. 135**).

Fig. 134

5. You can now *name* the group in the top left-hand corner if you wish (or call it Group 1). Click OK. You'll notice that all of your chosen tracks will now indicate their group in the channel fader (see **Fig. 136**).

Now that all of your tracks are in the same group, you'll find that you can hit the Mute button once to mute all of them, and if you start moving one of their faders, all of the faders for the tracks in that group will move. You can create multiple groups as a way of divvying up all of your tracks. You can also have an Instrument that is in multiple groups. Lastly, you can always go back to the Groups dialog box and edit which tracks are in which groups. I would suggest chiefly using Groups to mute multiple tracks at once when you're working on final mixes.

Fig. 135

Fig. 136

Changing the Color of Tracks

If you have a song with lots of audio tracks, you may not want them all to appear blue in the Mix window. You can change the color of any track.

1. Go to the Mix window, and select a track by its name (at the bottom of the fader).

2. Then go to Window>Color Palette in the main Pro Tools menu at the top. This window appears (see **Fig. 137**).

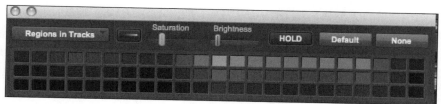

Fig. 137

3. From the drop-down menu you see in the top left of that dialog, change it from Regions in Tracks to Tracks, using the down arrow, then choose a color. Close the window. The track(s) you selected can then stand out a bit more in your Mix window (see **Fig. 138**).

Fig. 138

Automating Volume

The ability to draw in volume lines on each of your tracks to effectively automate your mix was covered in the earlier section of this guide called "Basic Automation of Audio Volume Levels." Take another look at that section, since when you're working with multiple tracks it's critical to save some of the headaches of running a final mix.

Alternatively, you can record the movement of your faders in the Mix window with a mouse. Refer to your Pro Tools documentation for more information on recording automation.

Finishing Off Your Mix—The Final Touches

Accompanying this section of the Teach Yourself Guide, you should watch tutorial movies #37 and #38 on the accompanying DVD—these follow the same steps that are being covered. In particular, consider adding a Master Fader to your session (see below).

Once you've gotten all your sounds together, you'll need to finalize your mix, add some automation if you need it, and bounce all your audio to one stereo file suitable for sharing or burning onto a CD.

Converting MIDI or Instrument Tracks to Audio

If you're triggering MIDI from a keyboard or some other external sound source (and not using the virtual instruments inside Pro Tools), at this stage you'll need to convert all MIDI tracks to audio tracks, or else you won't be able to get a proper final mix.

1. Create a new audio track (probably a single mono audio track) and physically connect the outputs from your MIDI source to your audio interface.

TIP If you want to create a stereo track of your synthesizer's playback, you may need to run two cables from the left/right outputs of the synth into two different inputs on your audio interface, if you have more than one input. Or take a mono signal from the synth and put this into a stereo track in Pro Tools.

2. You now need to send the audio from your module or keyboard into Pro Tools as *audio*, not MIDI. Record-enable the new track, press Record/Play, and let your entire song play through. the audio should get recorded as the synth's sounds are triggered via MIDI from the Pro Tools session playing.

3. When you're done, you can mute or remove the original MIDI track, which will now no longer be useful. You'll need to do this for all of the MIDI tracks in your session that trigger external devices.

4. With Instrument tracks, if you're using Xpand2 or another virtual instrument, Pro Tools will convert them to audio automatically for you when you bounce to disc. You do not need to do anything special to these tracks.

5. If you need to save computer memory, though, and are no longer planning to make any further changes to your MIDI data, you can choose to render your Instrument tracks as audio tracks—watch tutorial movie #26 for exact details.

Creating a Master Fader

Once you've recorded and mixed all your tracks to your liking, you may wish to create a master fader to ensure that all the tracks in your song will be controlled by the master fader from a *volume* standpoint. That way, at the end (or sometimes at the beginning) of the song, you can have one fader control all the volume levels of all the tracks, just like on a real mixing board.

All the tracks' outputs will automatically be sent to the master fader, assuming they are active and not muted. You do this the same way you create any new tracks.

1. Create a new track (using the normal shortcut). This time choose *one stereo Master Fader* from the dialog box. **Note:** If you choose a mono master fader, it probably won't work properly! This fader will be colored red in your Mix and Edit windows (see **Fig. 139**).

2. Notice in the Mix window that the master fader has no sends, but it does have inserts (meaning that you can insert audio plug-ins like EQ, reverb, and compression onto a master fader). Its output should naturally be set to output 1-2, the main stereo output of Pro Tools and its audio interface (see **Fig. 140**).

3. The master fader also has no panning controls and no input, since these would be unnecessary. All of that information is in the tracks themselves.

4. To check that your tracks are all linked to the master fader, go to the Mix window and watch your song play back. Play around with the fader on the red master fader track. You'll see that it now controls the whole song's volume level.

Fig. 139

5. Pay special attention to the level bar on the master fader. In order for your music to be clearly heard, it needs to have sufficient level. It can't exceed 0 dB, but it should come as close to that as possible.

6. If the overall volume level of your song is very low or needs some aural manipulation, consider adding a plug-in to the master fader, such as the Compressor/Limiter Dyn3

Fig. 140

in your included plug-in list. You would add this as an insert effect on the master fader itself. Refer to tutorial movie #38 for information on adding mastering tools as insert plug-ins on the master fader. Only use them if necessary, and with great care.

Note: A limiter is a device that limits the dynamic peaks in an audio file. This changes the natural character of your audio and enhances the overall volume at the expense of natural dynamics. Classical/acoustic music may be naturally lower in volume, and adding a limiter will make the music sound very "squashed" and artificial. Let your ears be your final guide as to how much limiting to use—louder is not always better, and compressor/limiters can ruin a perfectly good mix.

Adding a Fadeout for a Whole Song with the Master Fader

Since the master fader itself has no audio regions in it, you can't apply a fade the same way we learned earlier with regions. You have to use volume automation instead, and this is done in the Edit window.

1. Notice that the master fader, when viewed in the Edit window, is *already* being displayed as a volume line only (see **Fig. 141**).

2. To add a fadeout to the whole song, find the two places where the fade should *start* and *end*, select the Pencil tool, and *click* two points in the volume line, like this (see **Fig. 142**).

Fig. 141

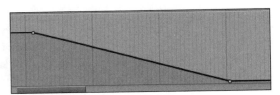

Fig. 142

3. There is no need to click and drag to create multiple points when you're using the Pencil tool. This method gives you a pretty smooth fadeout. Check that you chose the right fade length in the right place in the song. Use the Smart tool to reposition the points you created if necessary.

Bouncing to Disk

The process of creating a final mix in Pro Tools is called a "bounce." This usually renders your song as a *stereo interleaved* track, and that mix will be saved as a separate audio file in the file format AIFF on Mac and WAV on Windows. Note that Pro Tools by default does not export your mix as an MP3 file—use programs like iTunes to do that instead.

The biggest mistake you can make when you bounce your track to disk is to select too much or too little of your song. If you have any tracks muted, they won't be included in the final bounce. If your song has silence at the beginning, and you rewind to zero before bouncing, Pro Tools will play from the beginning when you start the bounce.

TIP It is crucial to select exactly the portions of your song that you wish to bounce, and to make sure you don't have empty space at the end of the mix.

See the example given below (see **Fig. 143**).

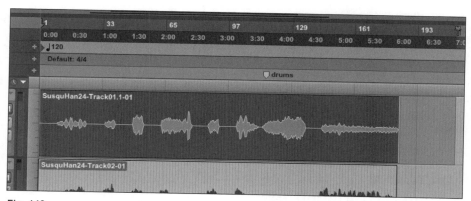

Fig. 143

You may have to zoom in to choose *exactly* the right place where your mix should start and end, and zoom out to ensure that all musical material has been included. Even though only one region is selected in Fig. 143, the whole song will play, as long as any tracks are not muted. This is a very common mistake that people make when they first bounce to disk. Notice also that the selection made above extends beyond the end of the first track's region. That's fine if there is musical content elsewhere that needs to make the final mix. Some tracks may end early.

1. Once your song sounds exactly the way you want and you're happy with it, go to the File menu and choose Bounce >To Disk, or use the shortcut: Command + Option + B (Mac) or Control + Alt + B (Windows). The following dialog box will appear (see **Fig. 144**).

2. The options you choose are very important, especially the *format*. Pro Tools chooses Multiple Mono by default, which is *not* what most people need most of the time. Change this choice to *Stereo Interleaved*—this

way it will create one stereo file, which is a stereo mix. The other choices will not give you this. Note also that Pro Tools does not create an MP3 file unless you have an extra plug-in on your computer—it will create either an AIFF or a WAV file.

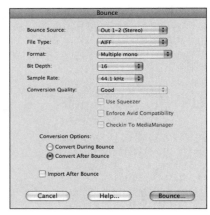

Fig. 144

3. When you click *Bounce* it will ask you in the next window to name the file—choose the *location* carefully where this final mix is to be stored!

Pro Tools cannot burn a CD directly; make sure that you bounce each song individually if you're working with multiple files, and then burn them to CD in a separate program. Note also that Pro Tools bounces your track in real time! You have to wait and listen for it to play all the way through, as it renders your session as a finished stereo file. You can stop the bounce in the middle if something sounds wrong.

Working with Video to Create a Movie/TV Soundtrack

Accompanying this section of the Teach Yourself Guide, you should watch tutorial movies #39 and 41 on the accompanying DVD—these follow the same steps that are being covered.

Pro Tools allows you to drag and drop any video straight into a session and start working with it (although you can't edit video with regular Pro Tools LE—you will need extra plug-ins like the DV Toolkit if you need to do video editing). Your soundtrack should fit the exact length of the movie. A good movie format to use when working with Pro Tools is QuickTime (.mov). There are plenty of good resources on the Internet for locating movies to use. Some are included with this curriculum guide.

Creating a movie soundtrack gives you the chance to mix audio and Instrument tracks, and experiment with many of the skills you have already acquired. This is ideal for teaching the idea of broadcasting and podcasting. There are no extra technical skills required beyond what has already been covered, but some skills, such as how to nudge and how to automate volume levels, will be especially useful.

1. Start a new blank Pro Tools session. Go to File>Import>Video and locate a video to use. A short one is good to start with.

2. Once you've chosen a video, an Import dialog box will appear, with an option to import any audio that might already be in the movie (see **Fig. 145**).

Fig. 145

The video file formats supported by Pro Tools can be made to appear in the Import dialog box. On a Mac, this is what you will see (see **Fig. 146**).

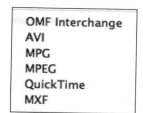

OMF Interchange
AVI
MPG
MPEG
QuickTime
MXF

Fig. 146

If you choose to import audio from the movie, and there is audio, it will be imported as a separate audio track which you may or may not choose to use.

3. At this point, the movie appears in your timeline, with a larger viewing screen also floating in the Edit window. This can be resized. Click Play to watch the movie, and note how long it lasts on the timeline. You may wish at this stage to have the Smart tool and Slip mode engaged.

4. Zoom in horizontally in the Edit window to take a closer look. The movie's frames will be displayed in greater detail as you do this (see **Fig. 147**).

Fig. 147

5. You may at this stage want to locate key moments in the movie and add markers (see earlier in the guide). This may help you later as you compose a soundtrack.

6. Don't forget that you can also select any point in the movie (if you have the Smart tool engaged) and then use the Nudge feature (covered earlier in the guide) to move slowly through the frames of the movie to see exactly when an action occurs. The shortcut to use the Nudge feature is simply to use the plus or minus buttons on your computer's numeric keypad. You can adjust your nudge settings at the top of the Edit screen.

7. You'll probably want to display all your timings in the Transport window as minutes and seconds until you have established a soundtrack, when you can switch to using bars and beats. It's up to you.

8. Open the Mix window. You'll notice that the video doesn't have its own track slider, because it has no sound.

Key Elements Needed to Make a Movie Soundtrack

A movie soundtrack comprises three elements:

1. Voiceover/dialogue

2. Sound effects

3. Musical backing track(s)

How you create these is up to you. Assuming you don't violate any copyrights, you can import audio into this session following all the steps learned earlier.

1. You can write a voiceover script, record it, and edit it, using the skills acquired earlier.

2. You can use Instrument tracks in Pro Tools (Xpand2 features lots of sound effect presets).

3. You can record your own musical backing track using any number of tracks.

All of these steps are identical to what was learned earlier. You just have to be aware that *everything should be subservient to what is happening in the movie.*

Voiceover and Dialogue Tracks

Bear in mind the excellent feature discussed earlier in this guide called Strip Silence, which allows you to quickly remove unwanted noise from voiceover tracks. Tutorial movie #40 covers this topic.

Get into the habit of cutting your vocal track into smaller parts so there are plenty of gaps in between speech, unless you only have a short amount of time in the movie to fit your voiceover. You may need to use the excellent TCE tool to squeeze or contract the audio.

Sound Effects

There are lots of sound effects that you can download from the Internet as small audio files if you don't wish to create your own using a virtual instrument.

Musical Backing Track(s)

When you are recording or assembling a video soundtrack, it's likely that you will use many different regions and sounds, along with a dialogue, or voiceover, track. Therefore, review how to perform fades, covered earlier in this guide. Some sounds will fade in and out. Listen to examples of TV programs, movies, and documentaries for reference.

TIP   Make sure that the AZ button is selected on the right-hand side of the Edit window, and use the shortcut letter D to fade in at the start of a region, and G to fade out at the end of a region. Always select the point in the region where the fade-in should go, or the point toward the end of a region where the fade-out should start.

Crossfades may also be appropriate—review how they are done.

A possibly more important technique is automating the volume level of each region so you don't have to manually adjust volume levels multiple times, and so your final bounce can be a painless one with no surprises!

TIP   You can change the view of any track in the Edit window from waveform to volume, on the left-hand side where the track is named. Use the Pencil tool (not the Smart tool) to draw the volume level of each track as a series of points in the timeline. You can edit the points later when the Smart tool is reactivated.

Don't forget to zoom in horizontally on your session to view small details! You can always zoom back out at any time, including while the session is playing.

Bounce to QuickTime Movie

When you are finished creating a soundtrack for your movie that contains all the elements described above, you're ready to render the whole session as a finished product.

1. Follow the same advice given in the previous section about bouncing a normal audio mix to disk. This time go to File>Bounce to>QuickTime Movie (assuming you want to render both the movie and the soundtrack you created together as one file). If you just need to create a file of the soundtrack (and join the movie to it later), choose Bounce to Disk instead.

2. As mentioned before, be *very* careful to select all the material you want included in the final mix. If tracks are muted, they won't be included!

3. If your audio lasts longer than the video in the timeline, it needs to be cut to the exact length of the movie, with a fade applied at the end if necessary, or it will not sound professional. Zoom in very closely to check that everything ends at the same point. No one wants to watch a movie where the picture has ended but the music is still playing, unless you have movie titles at that stage!

4. Bear in mind that you will not be able to see the finished movie play when you select *Bounce to QuickTime Movie*. You must wait until it is done, locate where you stored your bounce, and then watch it to ensure that everything sounds the way you want. You may have to bounce your session again after making a change to your soundtrack, until you have what you need.

Conclusion

Learning how to do all these things will allow you to create your own video broadcasts. Remember that the golden rule for creating great soundtracks is the following question: *Does the soundtrack you have created (including the dialogue), match and enhance what is going on in the movie?*

Part Three

Pro Tools Curriculum

Introduction
Structure for Each Module

The six modules adhere to the following layout:

1. Overview/time allocation
2. Topics covered
3. Skills acquisition tutorial videos
4. Prior knowledge (theory/experience)
5. Shortcuts to know (see below)
6. Golden Rules to know
7. Textbook references (see below)
8. Example sessions, audio, video, or MIDI data to use
9. Free additional resources available
10. Other materials/equipment needed
11. Procedures
12. Student assignment details
13. Assessment/learning outcomes
14. Extension topics, if required

For shortcuts to know (item 5), please refer to the shortcuts for Windows and Mac that are given later in this introduction. This is by no means a complete list of all Pro Tools shortcuts; this guide only suggests some key ones worth learning. The complete list of Pro Tools shortcuts is available as a separate 46-page PDF, so bear in mind that only some shortcuts are highlighted in these materials. In each module, important shortcuts should be reviewed, used, and learned.

For extra assistance with learning shortcuts, you can buy a Pro Tools custom keyboard for the Mac at www.kbcovers.com. For Windows or Mac users, certain websites offer Pro Tools keyboard stickers to attach to your computer keyboard. See www.editorskeys.com/Audio-Editing-Keyboards/pro-tools.html for an example. Check that these fully represent the shortcuts in Pro Tools 8, and that they work for Windows.

In terms of textbooks to use (item 7), there are several worth having for teaching, and some that could serve as a classroom book for all students to use (references to these are given in the lessons):

The Everything Guide to Digital Home Recording by Marc Schonbrun. Available through retailers. Go to marcschonbrun.com and click on Publishing, or search online for a copy. Marc's book is an incredible value for the money, and explores all the basics you need to know. Especially check out the newest edition (not yet released as of this writing), as it has been considerably updated with all the latest technology. The textbook references I give in the modules below are to both the existing book and its updated version.

Music Theory for Computer Musicians and ***Composition for Computer Musicians***, by Michael Hewitt (Cengage Learning). These two books take an interesting approach. The *Music Theory* book links the notation-based approach to music theory with what you might actually see in the piano-roll-type window that sequencers often use. It is strictly focused on music theory (scales, chords, etc.), and thus is outside the scope of these curriculum materials, but if you are planning on spending time talking with students about actual musical concepts and applying these to a sequencing environment, this is the book for you.

The *Composition* book is also mostly about the MIDI sequencing environment (which we cover in Module Three), but has more specific suggestions about how to use sequencing features to achieve a compositional effect. There's plenty of information about writing in a MIDI environment for drums, rhythm instruments, percussion, and dance music (pp. 15–73), rather than the approach taken with these Pro Tools materials, which is largely to use existing audio loops. Both are valid approaches, and both should be explored given enough time with students. The second half of the *Composition* book focuses a lot on writing and recording with acoustic instruments, and covers effects you'd find in an audio sequencer (chapter 10) and mixing (chapter 19). There's also plenty about how to write for specific instruments, so this book is worth using for several of the modules.

In terms of teacher references, you should definitely look at the **Hal Leonard Recording Method** series by Bill Gibson. This includes books on the following topics:

Microphones & Mixers

Instrumental & Vocal Recording

Recording Software & Plug-ins

Sequencing Samples & Loops

Engineering & Producing

Mixing & Mastering

Also check out **The Art of Mixing** by David Gibson. Here the author takes a unique, psychoacoustical approach to mixing by creating incredible graphic images of actual mixes (so students can visualize what a mix looks like). Scan these pictures and blow them up on a large screen for students to see and discuss while they listen to musical examples.

Guerrilla Home Recording by Karl Coryat. In this very readable book, the author talks about how to get great sound from any studio. It includes the following useful chapters:

"Chapter 3: The Signal Chain" (ideal for Modules Two, Four, and Five)

"Chapter 6: Effects" (ideal for Modules Two, Four, and Five)

"Chapter 8: Humanizing drum patterns and sequencers" (ideal for Module Three)

"Chapter 10: Mixing and Mastering" (ideal for Modules Five and Six)

You may find other resources available online, especially when it comes to real-world skills like microphone placement or the basics of audio effects.

List of Modules

The six modules, which can be considered somewhat independent of each other, include:

1. Getting familiar with Pro Tools

2. Editing stereo audio

3. Introduction to MIDI and Instrument tracks

4. Recording new audio

5. Learning to mix

6. Working with video and creating film/TV soundtracks

If you are unsure of your skill level as a teacher before embarking on this curriculum, definitely work your way through the Teach Yourself Pro Tools section first. You might also want to work with that section with your students in conjunction with the six modules.

In some schools, if there is very limited opportunity to create your own audio (either due to space or lack of instruments/microphones/students who can play or perform), then clearly Module Four will be a problem. However, there are plenty of sample files available with this guide that you can use.

With all the modules, a wealth of material is supplied, and in some cases, additional materials can be downloaded for free. The lack of a full recording environment in your school is not a major disadvantage. You'll soon want to equip your course with some extra materials—see the section "Other Equipment You May Need" later in this introduction.

Musical Content to Use with the Lessons

Bear in mind that the modules included here do not go into the basics of music composition or music theory. Students should of course learn the basics of harmony, melody, intervals, scales, and form, either before or during the time they spend learning Pro Tools.

There are also several excellent music software programs that will help in this process, such as Auralia (ear training lessons and practice) and Musition (music theory for drill and practice/assessment). For more details, visit www.risingsoftware.com or consult a good music technology retailer.

There are plenty of online resources to assist you, but please be careful not to break copyright laws. For example, for Modules One and Two (working with basic stereo audio), you can use the audio supplied, record audio of your school's ensembles (or have the students record it themselves), or you can find public domain audio on various websites. A great example of public domain audio is www.redhotjazz.com, which has an enormous amount of early jazz recordings from the 1920s.

If in doubt about copyright, steer clear of any sites that feature recent music, especially from the past 75 years. Consult Jim Frankel's excellent book *The Teacher's Guide to Music, Media, and Copyright Law* (available at www.halleonard.com). See also the section later in this introduction called "Copyright Issues."

For audio loops, use the huge number of loops from Big Fish Audio that ship with Pro Tools 8. You'll find these on your Pro Tools installation discs, and they take up around 8 GB of space on your drive if you load them all.

When working with MIDI information in Module Three, you can join (for free) a website called www.prs.net, which has thousands of MIDI files of classical music that can be downloaded and used with Pro Tools.

For Module Five, quite a few sessions are included that contain multitrack recordings (raw data from a CD I recorded a few years ago). Feel free to use these (or of course, have the students record their own multitrack sessions).

For Module Six, go to www.archive.org and download some of the thousands of ready-made silent movies and other older movies, which are ideal for use with film projects. Other suggestions for websites can be found in that module. In terms of file formats for movies, QuickTime is recommended as the most accessible format for saving, storing, and sharing movies, since it is compatible with either Windows or Mac machines. Ensure that you are running the latest version of QuickTime Player (currently version 7 as of this writing). You can download it from www.apple.com/quicktime. This version is also recommended for watching the accompanying tutorial movies.

For sound effects (Module Six), you can either create them yourself using the instrument sounds in Xpand2, or you can check out the various websites that have free downloadable sound effects. One suggestion is pacdv.com/sounds/index.html, but you can perform an online search using the phrase "sound effects" to find more sites. Save the sound effects to your hard drive by right-clicking (Control-clicking on a Mac if you don't have a two-button mouse) on them.

Your school may prevent you from downloading software for security reasons, so be advised that you may need to download the files at home and bring them back to school on a burned CD/DVD, portable USB flash drive, or FireWire/USB hard drive.

Time Allocation for the Modules

Every school tends to have a different schedule, but if you assume that contact time with students is around 80 minutes per lesson, and that you meet two or three times a week, you should allow anything up to 75 discrete and separate lessons to complete all the modules successfully— there are 41 tutorial movies alone to go through and practice, and although some of these cover pretty simple things, you need to allow plenty of time for students to work on their projects as well.

When it comes to calculating the time you need to take, two things are regularly neglected:

First, allow students time to practice their Pro Tools skills (by watching all the tutorial movies that come with the modules and using the many available shortcuts), because learning something once really doesn't allow a skill to "sink in." Will the student remember this unaided the next day or next week? Proficiency in music software is no different from practicing a musical instrument. It also involves allowing students to truly *play* with a feature, and discover its fun, creative elements. When it comes to in-depth exploration of Pro Tools, don't be afraid to have students team up and present their findings to the rest of the class.

Second, allow time for students to share an assignment, critique it with the class, hear positive comments/feedback, and then return to their projects to make changes. Work on the basis that each project may need at least five iterations before it can be considered "finished."

Therefore, if students follow each module (with the exception perhaps of Modules One and Two, which are introductory), and complete an assignment for each one, each module (Three through Six) may take a month of work to complete.

The golden rule for each of the modules should be to spend around 40 percent of the time teaching the concepts behind the features and allowing students to practice and acquire the skills they need; 35 percent of the time on student assignments; and 25 percent of the time allowing students to present their work and receive feedback, critique, and assessment.

Working with Video

For video editing, you can buy QuickTime Pro for around $30, which includes several things that regular QuickTime won't allow, like basic cropping of videos, and conversion into a wide variety of formats (sometimes referred to as codecs) for sharing online.

For students who want to get more into video editing, there are several excellent resources available: Macs already have iMovie included in the iLife suite, and for Windows users there is Pinnacle Studio Plus 12, which offers an educational discount (price is around $60 per computer) if you buy multiple copies for a lab. Pinnacle is made by Avid, which also makes Pro Tools.

Other Equipment You May Need

Other than a computer with an installed copy of Pro Tools, we'd suggest the following extras:

MIDI Keyboard. This doesn't need to have onboard sounds; a silent keyboard controller is fine, and very much the wave of the future, since most software these days includes its own built-in sounds. M-Audio makes a huge variety of these, with differing sizes and features. A good choice as of this writing is a KeyRig 49—around $99 each if you buy 10 or more, or other silent keyboards like the Q49 from Alesis, or the smaller controller keyboards made by Korg and Akai. Almost all MIDI keyboards connect to a computer via a standard USB connection (check on the back of the keyboard). You'll also likely need to install a software driver to allow the computer to communicate with the keyboard. If you can't find a driver, go to the website of the keyboard manufacturer to download a recent copy. Older MIDI keyboards may not have USB, so you may need to use a USB-to-MIDI cable like the M-Audio UNO, and connect the keyboard to your computer this way instead of direct via USB. There is no difference between a direct USB connection and a USB-to-MIDI cable. Once your computer can communicate with the keyboard, Pro Tools can access it too.

Headphones. Your audio interface (typically the Mbox) will have a 1/4-inch headphone output as well as a stereo Monitor Out (Mon Out) on the back, which is ideal for connecting a pair of speakers. Try to avoid having students bring in their own earbuds/headphones, as these don't provide great audio playback unless they are expensive. We recommend decent headphones like the M-Audio Studiophile Q40. Advocate safe listening levels in your labs, as hearing damage from earphones is all too common.

Speakers/Monitors. For speakers/monitors, there's a huge variety to choose from, and remember that learning to mix is essential using speakers rather than headphones! Once again, M-Audio offers several good choices in their current Studiophile series, from AV 40 monitors through the BX5a Deluxe monitors up to more expensive choices.

Lab Controller. Check out the Korg G.E.C. (Group Education Controller) from www.soundtree.com, which allows the teacher to listen in and comment on student progress at each lab station. It has many other benefits in the sense of being an audio network for your classroom. If you go this route, then the headphones you choose should have a talkback microphone attached for students to use. Consult SoundTree for details.

Microphones. These are required for Module Four in particular. There are two main types of microphones: dynamic and condenser. You'll want your students to have exposure to both types. Condenser microphones require *phantom power* to work (your audio interface should have a 48V or phantom power button for these microphones). M-Audio offers a range of condenser microphones at several price points—see www.m-audio.com for details. For dynamic microphones there are lots of choices, including the Shure SM57 and SM58, which can be found in almost every studio on earth. Microphones need special cables, called XLR cables. Make sure you have these on hand.

Instruments. Any acoustic or electric instrument can be recorded into Pro Tools. You'll need a stand for each microphone you plan on using. For electric guitar, amp-modeling boxes are available, which work via headphones. These devices send their signal straight into your audio interface without the need for a guitar amplifier. Popular examples include the Korg Pandora series, the TC Electronic Nova System, the Line 6 Pod, and the excellent Eleven Rack from Avid. It's important to know that an electric guitar won't sound great if you just plug it straight into your audio interface. Guitars need to go through a preamp stage to raise their volume to the proper level. All of the modeling devices mentioned in this paragraph act as a preamp. The alternative (discussed in the tutorial movies) is to plug your guitar straight into the audio interface and use the virtual amp simulation software in Pro Tools, called Eleven Free.

Blank CDs. Or some other way of storing/sharing work—an obvious thing, but please be sure to back up your work! This is especially true in lab environments. You can encourage students to bring flash drives to store their work and bring it home. Flash drives hold much more than CD-Rs, and are inexpensive.

Teacher Station. We recommend the teacher have the most advanced equipment in the room. Bear in mind that if you start doing multitrack recording (Modules Four and Five), you need to make an important decision: Do you want to record several sound sources simultaneously and have the tracks all come up separately in Pro Tools? If so, you need an audio interface with more than two inputs, such as the Digi 003 Factory or 003 rack. If you want to capture many sound sources simultaneously and then send a *stereo mix* of these into Pro Tools via your audio interface, then you may need to get a basic analog mixer. These mixers allow multiple devices to be connected to them (guitars, microphones, keyboards, etc.), and feature a stereo output on the back that you feed into your Mbox or other audio interface. An 8-channel mixer starts at around $100. The teacher station should also have studio-quality speakers. You want to be able to have the entire class hear students' work.

File Sharing Services. With this obvious need, www.yousendit.com is the best resource for you to use. It is free, and allows (as of this writing) files of up to 100 MB to be sent to anyone via e-mail. Because most e-mail servers don't allow attachments of more than 5 MB at a time, services like Yousendit are a great way to share files. If you're using a Mac, consider opening a MobileMe account, which allows you to share files.

Upload Sites and Mentoring. You may want to explore the idea of creating a virtual webspace for student projects to be uploaded in a secure manner. One great resource is www.wikispaces.com. Your school system may already have agreements with some of these types of providers. You can also have students interact with real-world composers to provide feedback on students' work. A great case study in online mentoring is the award-winning www.vtmidi.org website (which uses a notation view powered by Sibelius/Scorch as well as www.noteflight.com). The more students can be mentored on their creativity in a positive and substantive manner, the better. Mentors can also be other students with prior experience, teachers, and professionals in the field. A mixture of opinions is great to have.

Copyright Issues

Copyright is tricky. The simple rule is that whenever possible, students should create and use their own materials. The files supplied with this guide (including MP3 files, audio files, MIDI files, and Pro Tools session files) can be used freely.

The Big Fish Audio loops that are supplied with the Pro Tools software can also be freely used, as can the sounds generated by Xpand2, the onboard synthesizer/MIDI/sample playback engine that comes with Pro Tools.

Wherever possible in the lessons, I have suggested legal websites from which you can download materials, but in some cases there are gray areas. When in doubt, it's better to be safe than sorry.

For movies (Module Number Six), I have listed sites where you can download famous movie trailers. There is no problem having students edit and work with this material in an educational context. As long as the material is not posted publicly, you're not infringing on copyright.

Also note that music follows public domain rules (cut-off dates after which music enters the public domain). See www.pdinfo.com/index.php for more information. Current pop music of any kind is illegal to download, either in audio form or as a MIDI file. I have provided links to various sites where free music or sound effects may be downloaded. In general, stick to educationally valid websites such as www.prs.net and www.archive.org.

Listening Examples

Somewhat outside of the scope of these lessons, but no less critical, is the need to expose students to a wide variety of musical examples (real recordings) to help them understand more about recording techniques, as well as the history of recorded sound.

Listening examples should be played regularly to students so that they can develop critical listening skills as well as the ability to discuss constructively what they hear, what they may like or dislike, and how a sound might have been produced or recorded in the first place. This process has many benefits—you can use it as an opportunity to discuss the form and structure of songs, interesting instrumentation or harmony/melody, and the possible groundbreaking aspects of particular songs.

You can also take the opportunity to expose students to a much wider range of music than they were previously aware of, which should impact what they create themselves.

Lastly, you can and should have students keep a journal of what they listen to each week.

Play each musical example several times, and follow these steps:

1. Have students explain what they hear in a stream-of-consciousness way first. Then have them indicate specifically what they're hearing (instruments, chords, melody, or any musical things they notice).

2. Then talk about the form/structure of the song if it is notable or appropriate.

3. Then talk about why the particular piece is groundbreaking or worth knowing. Have students engage in positive critique at all times.

Taking the time to do this will pay great dividends when students start to compose and perform themselves.

Creating a Written Test for Students

You can create a written test at the end of each module, at the halfway point (a mid-term), or at the end of the year.

The next several pages provide a range of open-ended questions that are appropriate for each module. Feel free to use these when creating tests for your students. A good source for more in-depth descriptions, features, and knowledge is the Pro Tools Reference Guide, which is a PDF file found in the Pro Tools Help menu. Since this reference guide is over a thousand pages long, you'll want to use the search feature to find a feature or function in the program that you or your students don't understand.

Module One Example Questions

1. Name five things that you would change in the Pro Tools windows/screens to make editing/working easier.

2. To cut a region cleanly, what steps would you take?

3. Name and explain the five different types of tracks that you can create in Pro Tools.

4. Why might you use markers in Pro Tools?

5. Name some easy ways of making a copy of a region somewhere else in your track.

6. What is the spot edit mode for?

7. What does the Scrub tool do?

Module Two Example Questions

1. What color is an audio track in Pro Tools?

2. In the EQ screen in Pro Tools, what does the Q control do?

3. If you've inserted reverb on a track, how do you hear the track without reverb?

4. What is hard-knee compression?

5. How do you quantize the audio of a drum loop that you've imported, using Elastic Time?

6. How do you insert a tempo change in Pro Tools?

7. What does shuffle edit mode do?

Module Three Example Questions

1. What happens when you open a MIDI file in Pro Tools, and how do you make it play back using the sounds inside Pro Tools?

2. How do you create a click track in Pro Tools, and why would you create one?

3. Which edit mode is best to use when working with time-sensitive MIDI material?

4. How many different subdivisions of a single quarter note are there in Pro Tools by default?

5. What does quantization do?

6. Give specific examples of when you would quantize MIDI data and when you would not.

7. Describe two main ways that you could make a MIDI or Instrument track get gradually louder/softer on playback.

8. How do you change the title of your piece when you're in the notation view window of a MIDI/Instrument track?

Module Four Example Questions

1. How would you mic a drum kit?

2. If your audio interface only has two inputs for microphones, how do you record a band with multiple microphones (more than two)?

3. What is "proximity effect"?

4. Describe track compositing in Pro Tools and how it works.

5. How do you make a session scroll as it plays in Pro Tools?

6. What is sample rate and sample resolution?

7. What are the pros and cons of recording at higher sample rates?

Module Five Example Questions

1. When would you use AudioSuite in Pro Tools?

2. Describe how to set up an auxiliary send for reverb and why you would do this.

3. How would you ensure that several (not all) tracks in your final mix all faded out at the same time?

4. What is normalization?

5. Describe why you might create a master fader for mixdown.

6. If you were using delay as an effect on a Pro Tools session running at a speed of 120 bpm, what would be an obvious delay time to use (in milliseconds)? Show how you calculate your answer.

Module Six Example Questions

1. What video format is best to use with Pro Tools?

2. How do you convert a YouTube video into something you could use with Pro Tools?

3. In video, what is meant by the term "codec," and what factors are involved in choosing a codec?

4. Why is it a good idea to add markers to a session that contains video?

5. Which of the edit modes might be best to use when synchronizing sound to onscreen action in a video?

6. If Pro Tools doesn't seem to play from where you have selected in a track, which icon or feature do you need to ensure is selected?

7. Before bouncing your whole session to a QuickTime movie or disk, what things should you make sure you have done to your whole session first?

Useful Shortcuts to Learn for Each Module (Mac and Windows)

Listed below are both sets of shortcuts for Mac and Windows. Shortcuts refers to holding down modifier keys along with the other listed keys. Mac shortcuts are in parentheses after the Windows shortcuts.

Below are standard modifier keys for Windows and their Mac equivalents:

Windows	Mac OS X
Control key	Command key
Alt key	Option key
Shift key	Shift key
Start key	Control key

Shortcuts for Module One

Windows	Mac	Function
Spacebar (or 0 on numeric keypad)	Spacebar (or 0 on numeric keypad)	Play/stop session
Shift + Spacebar	Shift + Spacebar	Play back at half speed
Control + =	Command + =	Open/close Mix window
Alt + ;	Opt + ;	Open/close Workspace window
Alt + drag region	Opt + drag region	Paste region
Control + Z	Command + Z	Undo
Control + drag icon	Command + drag icon	Reposition icons at top of screen
Control + Shift + I	Command + Shift + I	Import audio
Tilde (~) or Accent (`) key	Tilde (~) or Accent (`) key	Toggle between the four edit modes
Escape key (Esc)	Escape key (Esc)	Toggle between the seven tools
Alt + 1–4 (main)	Opt + 1–4 (main)	Switch between the four edit modes
Control + 1–7 (main)	Command + 1–7 (main)	Switch between the seven tools
0 on numeric keypad	0 on numeric keypad	Play/stop from cursor selection
1 on numeric keypad	1 on numeric keypad	Move playback line back one bar
2 on numeric keypad	2 on numeric keypad	Move playback line forward one bar
4 on numeric keypad	4 on numeric keypad	Turn on/off loop playback
Control + ([) or (]) keys	Command + ([) or (]) keys	Zoom horizontally on selection
Start + up/down arrows	Control + up/down arrows	Zoom vertically on selection
Control + Shift + N	Command + Shift + N	Start a new track within the session
Control + Shift + W	Command + Shift + W	Close current session

Control + Option + B	Command + Option +B	Bounce selected audio to a stereo file
Plus/Minus (numeric keypad)	Plus/Minus (numeric keypad)	Nudge selection forward/ backward
Alt + R	Opt + R	Repeat selection
Alt + H	Opt + H	Shift selection
Control + E	Command + E	Separate region (split in two)
Control + H	Command + H	Heal separation of selected regions
Enter (on numeric keypad	Enter (on numeric keypad	Add/name marker at selection
Control + 5 (number pad)	Command + 5 (number pad)	View all marker points
Control + F	Command + F	Create definable crossfade

Extra Shortcuts That Work If the A/Z Button (the Keyboard Focus Button) Is Highlighted

(Top Right of the Tracks Viewable Area)

Click a point in a region and type D	Fade up from the beginning
Click a point in a region and type G	Fade out to the end
Select a region and type R	Horizontally zoom in
Select a region and type T	Horizontally zoom out
Select a region and type E	Toggle height of selected region(s)
Select a region and type P	Move up to the track above
Select a region and type :	Move down to the track below
The letter A	Trim region to the left of selection
The letter L	Return play position to beginning
The keys < and >	Nudge selected region left or right
The numbers 1–5 (main numbers)	Toggle between various zooms

Shortcuts for Module Two

Windows	Mac	Function
1 (on numeric keypad)	1 (on numeric keypad)	Rewind (also while playing)
2 (on numeric keypad)	2 (on numeric keypad)	Fast forward (also while playing)
Enter key (Return key)	Enter key (Return key)	Go to session start
Double-click on a region	Double-click on a region	Name a specific region
Shift + M	Shift + M	Mute selected track/region
Shift + S	Shift + S	Solo selected track/region
Control + N	Command + N	Start a new session
Control + O	Command + O	Open an existing session
Control + S	Command + S	Save existing session
Control + L	Command + L	Lock a region (prevent it from moving

Shortcuts for Module Three

Windows	Mac	Function
Start + =	Control + =	MIDI piano-roll editor
Start + Alt + =	Control + Alt + =	Score view/editor
Alt + =	Opt + =	MIDI event list
Alt + 0 (main numbers)	Opt + 0 (main numbers)	Quantization screen
Alt + 1 (numeric keypad)	Opt + 1 (numeric keypad)	Time operations window
Alt + 2 (numeric keypad)	Opt + 2 (numeric keypad)	Tempo operations window
Alt + T	Opt + T	Transpose selected MIDI
Alt + P	Opt + P	Change duration of selected notes
Alt + Y	Opt + Y	Select/split notes

Shortcuts for Module Four

Windows	Mac	Function
3 (numeric keypad)	3 (numeric keypad)	Record
Alt + L (or 5 on numeric keypad)	Opt + L (or 5 on numeric keypad)	Loop Record
Alt + ;	Opt + ;	Open/close Workspace browser
Control + 1 (numeric keypad)	Command + 1 (numeric keypad)	Show/hide Transport window

Shortcuts for Module Five

Windows	Mac	Function
Control + Start + Alt + Up/down arrows	Command + Option + Control + Up/down arrows	Fit all tracks into Edit window
Control + G	Command + G	Create a group
Control+ Start + [	Command+ Control + [	Zoom to see complete session

Shortcuts for Module Six

Windows	Mac	Function
Control + Alt + Shift + I	Command + Opt + Shift + I	Import video into Pro Tools
Control + U	Command + U	Strip Silence from audio
Control + 9 (numeric keypad)	Command + 9 (numeric keypad)	Show/hide video window
Control + Q	Command + Q	Quit Pro Tools

Skills Acquisition Tutorial Movies

(Included on Accompanying Disc)

1. Starting Pro Tools and making setup changes
2. Customizing the screen and the three main Pro Tools windows
3. Importing audio
4. The four edit modes
5. The seven tools
6. Zooming horizontally and vertically
7. Editing audio (repeat/consolidate/split/heal/paste/nudge regions)
8. Adding marker points in audio and quickly finding them
9. Fading audio in and out and crossfading
10. Basic automation of the volume levels of audio
11. Using the inserts for audio or instrument tracks
12. Adding or editing EQ
13. Adding or editing reverb
14. Adding or editing compression
15. The workspace
16. The Time Compression/Expansion tool in Pro Tools
17. Using pitch correction in Pro Tools
18. Using Elastic Time in Pro Tools
19. Creating a MIDI or Instrument track
20. Virtual instrument sounds in Pro Tools
21. The Xpand2 and Structure interfaces
22. Recording MIDI data and quantizing
23. Editing MIDI data (different views of data)
24. Time, tempo, and event operations

25. MIDI control change information

26. Rendering MIDI data as audio

27. Import/export of MIDI data

28. Setting up a track to record (monitoring)

29. Working with MIDI and audio in the same session

30. Overdubbing/drop-in recording

31. Using different takes (track compositing)

32. Navigating a multitrack session

33. Grouping tracks together

34. Creating an auxiliary input for reverb

35. Recording fader movements

36. AudioSuite plug-ins

37. Adding a master fader

38. Mastering tools for the final mix

39. Importing a movie and adding marker points

40. Working with strip silence for a voiceover track

41. Rendering as a QuickTime movie, and different video codecs

Modules

Module One: Getting Familiar with Pro Tools

Overview/Time Allocation

See student learning outcomes below. This first module is primarily designed to get students comfortable with how Pro Tools works, and allow students to customize their own workflows so they work fast and efficiently, employing a variety of shortcuts to help them learn the software. There are two assignments for the students to complete: the first based on editing a voiceover, and the second based on fading from one kind of audio stream into another. Allow between five and 10 classes of 90 minutes each to complete this module.

Topics Covered

- ▶ Pro Tools screens/timelines
- ▶ Starting a session and saving data
- ▶ Checking audio settings
- ▶ Importing audio
- ▶ Edit modes, the seven tools, and making selections
- ▶ Editing audio basics
- ▶ Fades and crossfades
- ▶ Altering the volume levels of audio using automation
- ▶ Bouncing audio

Skills Acquisition Tutorial Videos

The following movies include the skills you need: have students watch them one at a time, practice each one, and then move on to the assignment.

1. Starting Pro Tools and making setup changes

2. Customizing the screen and the three main Pro Tools windows

3. Importing audio

4. The four edit modes

5. The seven tools

6. Zooming horizontally and vertically

7. Editing audio (repeat/consolidate/split/heal/paste/nudge regions)

8. Adding marker points in audio and quickly finding them

9. Fading audio in and out and crossfading

10. Basic automation of the volume levels of audio

Prior Knowledge (Theory/Experience)

None, except some basic computer knowledge (programs/files/where to save/good computer habits)

Shortcuts to Know

Please refer to the shortcuts page at the end of the Introduction. Ensure that students attempt each shortcut, and try to start using as many as possible. Test students on these shortcuts at the end of each module.

Golden Rules to Know

1. By default, use the Smart Tool and Slip mode. Be aware of how the cursor changes its appearance as you move it over the audio (with the Smart Tool selected).

2. Turn off screens/timelines/settings you don't need.

3. Enable scrolling on playback from this menu: Options>Edit Window Scrolling>Page.

4. To play audio from a certain point, either use the forward/reverse buttons, or click on a region until you see a flashing cursor.

5. Hit the spacebar to play and stop a session (or learn alternative shortcuts).

6. Always be aware of what is selected in the session—this will affect playback and any editing that you do.

7. The easiest way to select nothing in your session is to press the Return to Start button in the floating Transport window (see **Fig. 1**).

Fig. 1

8. Pro Tools is nondestructive. You can recover any regions that have been edited from the regions list.

9. Zoom in/out as much and as often as you can—both horizontally and vertically.

10. When you separate a region, try and do it at a zero crossing point.

11. If you put a fade on a region, to remove it select it and press Delete.

12. To remove any markers in your score, select them and drag them off the timeline.

Textbook References

The new edition of Marc Schonbrun's book *The Everything Guide to Digital Home Recording* talks about the history of recording as well as the transition from analog to digital in chapters 1, 4, and 5. These chapters would be a good starting point for students to read and discuss.

Example Sessions, Audio, MIDI or Video Data to Use

Included with these lessons: voiceover audio files for importing into Pro Tools and a multitrack Pro Tools session in the folder called "Module One Jam."

Free Additional Resources Available

See the Introduction to these lessons under the section "Musical Content to Use with the Lessons."

Other Materials/Equipment Needed

None required for this module—just the software and a way to hear the audio (via headphones or speakers).

Procedures

1. Review the goal of this module (primarily to learn the ins and outs of the Pro Tools interface).

2. Review the topics.

3. Start by explaining some history behind recording on a computer (see Textbook References), and what came before this latest technology.

   How does a computer store digital audio and make a soundwave appear on screen?

   Can you tell whether a sound is loud or soft just by looking at it?

4. The 10 tutorial movies for this module are critical for students to watch and digest carefully. Students should watch each movie and then practice what they have learned. These are all the main components that will make them comfortable using Pro Tools, and once they have completed this stage, they can start being creative.

5. Use the example audio that comes with this module, and start with individual tracks so students can manipulate them without being confused by something else playing at the same time.

6. Review all the shortcuts students should know.

7. Review the golden rules they should have learned.

8. Move on to the assignments.

9. Give students time to play and comment on each other's assignments.

10. Evaluate the assessment criteria for all students; they can start by assessing themselves.

11. Review the extension topics for those students who are ready and able to move on.

Student Assignment Details

There are two slightly different assignments:

Assignment One

1. To edit a speech for a news program or radio advertisement to get only the key topics/points of the speaker and remove any unnecessary dialogue. The total length of the speech should be exactly 60 seconds from start to finish.

2. Have students start by creating an empty new Pro Tools session and importing several audio voiceover files (provided in the Module One files folder). Students should import each voiceover as a separate track.

3. Ask students to cut out regions from different tracks, copy/repeat regions, set markers in the audio, and bounce the whole session to a separate stereo file. The result should sound like one seamless, edited voiceover with no discernible gaps, bumps, or clicks in it.

4. The audio can fade from one voiceover into another if necessary (students should experiment with fading various bits of audio in and out, as well as dragging audio along the session timeline to reposition it).

5. Students should keep a log of what they did with this (and all) assignments, and what techniques they learned.

Assignment Two

1. To extend the length of an existing multitrack song. In this producer-style assignment, students will open the supplied multitrack session called "Module One Jam" (containing five tracks of audio that all play at once). Four of the tracks are in mono, and the drums are in stereo.

2. Students must extend this song (currently around 1:45) to 3:00 by carefully cutting and pasting the existing audio tracks using the editing skills they have acquired and watching the tutorial videos again if necessary.

3. Students may also want to experiment with the volume levels and panning of the tracks in the mixer, but they shouldn't start to add effects at this stage (that's reserved for Modules Two, Four, Five, and Six).

4. Note that the students should probably work in Grid mode and first attempt to calculate the actual speed of the song. **Teacher Hint:** *The actual tempo of the song is 102 bpm (beats per minute) if students can't work this out.* The session says that the tempo is 120 bpm, but this is not the case with the audio that was originally recorded (you can tell if you go to Create>Click track, and add one in). Students should use the click track as a reference point.

    Note: *Be careful when adding a new tempo marker to the song; make sure that the song is right at the beginning and then click the tempo plus button to add a new tempo to the song and override what is already there.*

    Once students know the correct tempo of the song, it will be a lot easier for them to make edits that work smoothly. They can certainly try it without doing this, but the edits won't work as smoothly, and they should stay in Slip mode until they know the correct bpm of the song.

5. Students should also learn how to zoom in really close in the track to find good places to cut the regions. They may wish to experiment with the Repeat feature: Select a region and type Option + R (Alt + R in Windows) to repeat a region.

6. Students may remove some of the existing audio if they wish, and take only part of what they are given and expand upon this, but they should not record any fresh audio or import any extra audio into the session.

7. When editing is complete, students must bounce all the audio to a single stereo track, which should sound smooth and listenable. The final result should be no longer than three minutes. Students should compare against each other's work.

Assessment/Learning Outcomes

Students should be able to:

1. Understand the connections on the computer/interface/MIDI keyboard and the internal settings for Pro Tools.

2. Know how to start a Pro Tools session, where to save it and in what format.

3. Understand Pro Tools windows and be able to customize the screen.

4. Import and play back audio.

5. Explain the four edit modes and seven tools in Pro Tools.

6. Do basic editing of audio (cut/repeat/paste/fade).

7. Turn on loop playback and choose timeline selection points.

8. Export/bounce audio.

9. Know all the Pro Tools shortcuts listed above.

10. Share and describe what they have done in their assignments.

Extension Topics (If Required)

Students can download some extra audio files from various sources: perhaps from a free sound effects website or using the free audio examples at www.prs.net.

Alternatively, students can download the audio of famous speeches from the Internet, and build their own audio collage by editing and crossfading the audio pieces together. A great website for this is www.archive.org/details/audio.

Module Two: Editing Stereo Audio

Overview/Time Allocation

See student learning outcomes below. This second module is designed to have students learn basic sonic manipulation of audio (by exploring various audio plug-ins such as EQ, compression, and reverb), and also how to manipulate the timing aspects of audio (using the elastic time and pitch features in Pro Tools).

This module closely models what an audio engineer might do when editing a stereo recording of a concert or rehearsal to remove noise and improve or alter the sound. For the second aspect of this module, students will learn how to select different types of rhythmically sensitive audio (drum loops or loops of rhythmic playing) and match them together so that they work musically. No new recording of audio is required at this stage.

There are two assignments to complete. Allow between 10 and 15 classes of 90 minutes each to complete this module.

Topics Covered

1. Introduction to digital recording principles

2. Introduction to the signal path

3. Basic EQ

4. Basic compression

5. Basic reverb

6. Auditioning audio loops using the workspace window

7. Time stretching/pitch stretching (TCE tool/various plug-ins)

8. Elastic Audio (calculating/matching audio together)

Skills Acquisition Tutorial Videos

The following movies include the skills you need: have students watch them one at a time, practice each one, and then move on to the assignment.

11. Using the inserts for audio or Instrument tracks

12. Adding or editing EQ

13. Adding or editing reverb

14. Adding or editing compression

15. The Workspace window in Pro Tools

16. The Time Compression/Expansion tool in Pro Tools

17. Using pitch correction in Pro Tools

18. Using Elastic Audio in Pro Tools

Prior Knowledge (Theory/Experience)

Students should have completed Module One.

Shortcuts to Know

Please refer to the shortcuts page at the end of the Introduction. Ensure that students attempt each shortcut and start using as many as possible. Test students on these shortcuts at the end of each module.

Golden Rules to Know

1. It is always a good idea to audition audio in the workspace browser before importing it or dragging it into Pro Tools.

2. Take very careful note of the overall tempo of any Pro Tools session you work on—this is the basis of many of the calculations that Pro Tools will make.

3. Be aware of how to change the tempo of a session.

4. Use the metronome icon at the top of the workspace screen to audition audio in the actual tempo of the song you're working on.

5. Bear in mind that some audio will be harder for Pro Tools to process from an elastic perspective—concentrate on *rhythmic* analysis of audio (like drum loops or rhythmic guitar/bass riffs, etc.).

6. EQ is probably the most used of all the effects in a studio environment—be aware of how much EQ can alter the tonal quality of audio.

7. Ensure that you understand the signal path and what effects should be placed in what order.

8. Don't add too much reverb or compression—the general rule for effects is: "If you can hear it, you may have added too much."

9. Seek a second opinion from your fellow students!

Textbook References

The Everything Guide to Digital Home Recording covers the basics of EQ, reverb, and compression in chapters 15 and 16.

Chapter 10 of Michael Hewitt's book *Composition for Computer Musicians* also discusses how and why you would use effects like EQ, reverb, and compression, and also distinguishes between master effects and insert effects.

Example Sessions, Audio, MIDI or Video Data to Use

A stereo recording is provided for the first student assignment. You can also use the sample session provided with Module One if students want to start adding effects to that instead.

Loops from the Big Fish Audio Loops are required for the second assignment. A solo vocal example is available for use with the Extension task.

Free Additional Resources Available

A myriad of websites provide downloadable loops and material for students to edit and cut. You should probably download any audio for use with your class on a separate computer free from your school's network restrictions, and discourage students from trying to download anything on their computers at school. Make sure to download MP3 files or WAV files.

Here are some suggested websites to use:

- ► www.archive.org/details/audio
- ► www.freeaudio.org
- ► www.freeclassicaudiobooks.com
- ► www.americanrhetoric.com/top100speechesall.html
- ► http://librivox.org
- ► www.pdsounds.org

Other Materials/Equipment Needed

None required for this module—just the software and a way to hear the audio (via headphones or speakers).

Procedures

This module follows from Module One, and students should employ all the skills they have already learned, as well as learn how to add effects and how to work with elastic time.

1. Review the work done in Module One, as well as the goals of this module and the topics that will be covered, and discuss what might improve the quality of a recording beyond simply re-recording what has been done.

2. Talk about EQ, compression, and reverb, three of the central pillars of the recording industry. Discover more about these three effects using the textbook references or have students conduct their own online research.

   Can students clearly describe what each of these effects does?

   Why might each of these effects (EQ, compression, and reverb) be useful, and when would they be used?

3. Show how a DAW (digital audio workstation) is a replication of an analog mixing board. If you have an analog mixer, illustrate how similar it is to the layout of the mixer in Pro Tools. Talk about the *signal path*— the progression of an audio signal from a *raw* condition into an *effected* condition. Spend time looking closely at all the controls in the Mix window in Pro Tools.

4. Work through tutorial movies 11–14, and allow time for students to practice each of the skills on their own in Pro Tools. To do so, they will need to open an existing Pro Tools session or start a new blank one, and import audio into it each time. Ensure that you have these resources available. Files are included with this part of the module for students to use.

5. Review the shortcuts students will need to know and learn for this part of the module.

6. Review the golden rules for this part of the module.

7. At this point, students may want to try the first assignment for this module. After they have completed it, go through a critique and assessment of their work.

8. After the above is done, move on to the sections of this module concerning elastic time and pitch stretching. Start by talking about how it was impossible in the past to stretch the timing of audio without speeding up or slowing down its pitch. Why was this so? Talk about the tape-based world of recording (review textbook or online resources if necessary).

9. Discuss what might actually be happening when time-stretching a soundwave. What needs to happen physically if a soundwave is to play back slower or faster *without* its pitch changing?

10. To show or demonstrate the old tape-based way of stretching audio, open a Pro Tools session with some audio already in it, and solo and select a region so it is highlighted.

11. Then get the students to select the Scrub tool and press and hold their mouse over the audio as they move it back and forth; they will hear it slow down or speed up, very much like in the old days when one could manually slow down or speed up a tape recorder. The Scrub tool can be a good way of locating an exact point in a soundwave, such as for editing purposes.

12. Next, in the Pro Tools menu at the top of the screen, go to AudioSuite>Pitch Shift>Pitch Shift. The following window appears (see **Fig. 2**).

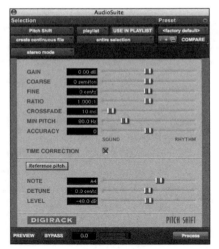

13. Press the Preview button (in the bottom left of the window), and the audio starts playing. As it plays, drag the slider that says Coarse to the left or right, and you'll hear the audio's pitch and speed slow down/speed up in specific increments. You can also use the Fine slider to make more narrow adjustments. Click on the Preview button to stop. This is a great effect for slightly altering the pitch of existing audio, but there may be a better way to manipulate audio. Close this window.

Fig. 2

Fig. 3

14. Next, show the Time Compression/Expansion Trimmer tool, which is the next best way of working: Select an audio region, and go to the Trimmer tool. Press and hold on it, and three choices appear. Choose TCE (see **Fig. 3**).

Now with this tool, move the cursor to the end of the region you have selected, and click and drag to the left or right. The audio will literally be squeezed or expanded. Play back the audio to hear what has happened. Pro Tools has attempted to process all of the soundwave and play it back at a different speed *without* altering the pitch. This is a supremely useful thing. Ask students to discuss when this might be an appropriate feature to use.

Talk about Elastic Time in Pro Tools, and how more science can be brought to bear on this technique, because the software can now effectively calculate the timing of an existing piece of rhythmic playing, and also pitch-correct a melody.

15. Now have students attempt the second assignment. They should learn two key things at this stage: How to audition drum loops using the workspace browser (see the tutorial movies); and how Pro Tools calculates the elastic analysis of a piece of audio for which we might not

immediately know the speed/bpm. It is certainly best to concentrate on audio that has a *rhythmic* element to it, since with some audio (like a solo melody) it may not be easy or possible for Pro Tools to calculate the timing. Using the supplied examples or the Big Fish Audio loops, ensure that students know how to use both of these methods.

16. Pitch correction is a task best left to the extension topic, although all students should watch tutorial movie #17 on this subject.

Student Assignment Details

There are two assignments:

Assignment One

1. The object of this assignment is to clean up some audio and add effects (using insert effects like EQ, compression, and reverb from the Mixer window) so the audio can be exported out of Pro Tools in a better-sounding condition as a finished stereo file.

2. This assignment can be done using a variety of audio sources. You can either use the sample session supplied with this lesson (which features a stereo live recording), use downloaded audio from some of the websites given above (see Free Resources), or use the same sample session from Module One.

3. Students may need to create separate regions, and then cut out the noise at the beginning and end. They should delete unwanted regions (although these will end up in the regions list, and can be retrieved later if needed).

4. Students should add a fade if necessary at the end of the song, and also apply some insert effects (EQ and maybe compression—or perhaps explore what some of the other effects in Pro Tools might do to improve the audio).

5. Lastly, students should bounce their finished audio to a stereo audio file. There should be no silence at the beginning or end of the track, and it should be ready for radio play or broadcast.

Assignment Two

1. This assignment concerns Elastic Time (the time stretching/matching of different pieces of audio so they play in time). The task is to create a

new blank session, choosing a tempo other than 120 bpm, and create a click track for that session— this will be the reference point for testing whether the song stays in time once audio loops are brought into the session.

2. Create a click track from the Create menu in Pro Tools. Then, using the Window>Workspace feature, have students audition several different loops from the Big Fish Audio loops folders. These need to have their elastic audio analysis done so it will be possible to stretch or squeeze these loops to fit the timing of the session. Watch the tutorial video to work out how this is done.

3. Students may also wish to explore using the TCE tool (Time Compression/Expansion Trimmer tool), although the more professional way to time-stretch their samples is via the elastic analysis option, as this gives you more control over all the transients in an audio loop. Again, the tutorial movies will explain more.

4. Once the audio has been imported and conforms to the timing of the session, continue the task using loops from the Big Fish Audio loops library (guitar, bass, and other loops are available). All loops, if they are essentially rhythmic, can easily be transformed to work with the timing/ speed of the song. Take care, though: swung loops (with triplet timing) may need more careful work, and also loops in 6/8 or 3/4 time may not work in a 4/4 song! Carefully review the videos on elastic time.

5. Lastly, students should import an extra track of audio (perhaps taking one of the guitar loops from the Big Fish Audio loops collection), and work on transposing the pitch of this audio (watch the pitch correction tutorial video for details on how this is done).

6. The finished song should have several different loops all playing in time together, with a decent audio balance between each track (use the Mixer to do this). The session should then be bounced down to a stereo audio mix without the click playing to demonstrate that students have mastered this technique.

Assessment/Learning Outcomes

Students should be able to:

1. Explain the basics of digital recording theory
2. Understand the principles and practice of using EQ

3. Understand the principles and practice of using reverb

4. Understand the principles and practice of using compression

5. Understand Elastic Time in Pro Tools

6. Do pitch correction of audio in Pro Tools

7. Use the workspace window in Pro Tools

8. Audition and match audio loops from a timing perspective

9. Know all the Pro Tools shortcuts listed above

10. Share and describe what they have done in their assignments

Extension Topics (If Required)

A good extension topic might be for students to work with pitch-correction software to attempt to fix the tuning of a vocal performance (or anything with a solo melody in it). This is what you might term Elastic Pitch, and it is somewhat related to Elastic Time—namely, the ability to alter the pitch of audio without altering its speed. In the old analog, tape-based environment, altering the pitch of audio usually resulted in a change in the speed of the audio (although you can still achieve this result using Elastic Time and Varispeed if you wish).

The two main companies that provide this software are Celemony (makers of Melodyne) and Antares (makers of Auto-Tune Evo). Both have demo versions that can be downloaded.

The technique of using pitch-correction software, especially on vocals, is now commonly used in pop and R&B songs, and is sometimes deliberately overused to lend a mechanical, vocoder-like feel to the whole vocal line instead of specifically fixing flat or sharp notes.

Note that Melodyne Essential is supplied as a free plug-in with Pro Tools 8 in the Ignition pack, but it can be somewhat difficult to use (it must be run in Rewire mode, and there are quite a few steps involved in making this work). The stand-alone demo versions of Melodyne or Auto-Tune are therefore recommended for the purposes of this extension task.

1. Download the demo versions of either Melodyne or Auto-Tune:

2. Celemony Melodyne: Go to www.celemony.com and click on Demo Versions on the left-hand side of the page, then choose Melodyne Studio for download.

3. Antares Auto-Tune Evo: Go to www.antarestech.com/download/ demoform.php

4. In the case of Melodyne, you should be able to download a stand-alone version of the software which, although non-saving, allows students to explore how to work with pitch-correction software and see what the interface looks like (see below).

5. Antares allows you to download an RTAS version of the plug-in, which will work inside of Pro Tools for 10 days before you must pay to authorize it. The Antares plug-in can be used by starting a Pro Tools session and importing the vocal audio file supplied with this module called Module Two Extension.aif. Then open the mixer, click on the inserts, and choose multi-channel plug-in>Pitch Shift >Auto-Tune Evo. The window looks like this (see **Fig. 4**).

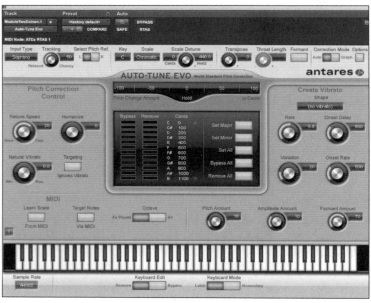

Fig. 4

6. Ask some students to explore how the plug-in works, and present their findings to the rest of the class.

7. For Melodyne, once the software is downloaded and installed, launch it (it doesn't need other software to be running on your computer), and from the File menu, open the vocal audio file supplied with this module

called Module Two Extension.aif. You should see the vocal appear graphically on the screen, and be able to play it back (see **Fig. 5**).

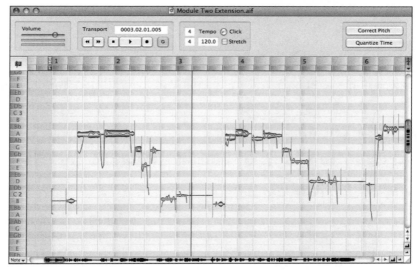

Fig. 5

8. If you experience problems playing the file, check the Preferences menu of the software to ensure that it is seeing your hardware device (typically the Mbox) for playback.

9. Students should be able to select any of the notes and move them up and down with their mouse—they could even rewrite the sung melody this way, which is a lot of fun. Note that the pitches are displayed on the left-hand side vertically and the timing is displayed horizontally.

10. In Module Three, the concept of *quantization* will be covered for MIDI data, but these software programs will do the same thing with actual audio pitches by altering a slightly out of tune note so that it snaps to the nearest half step. If you drag a note a long way out of its original position, it may start to sound quite inhuman!

11. The demo version of Melodyne may also emit a deliberate sine wave of interference if you select all the notes—Command + A (Mac) or Control + A (Windows)—and click the Correct Pitch button in the top right to correct the pitch of the whole piece!

12. As with Auto-Tune, students should explore the plug-in and then report their findings to the rest of the class.

13. Both Melodyne and Auto-Tune would like you to upgrade to full versions. This is money well spent if you plan to fix a lot of melodies! You can export audio from Pro Tools, fix it in these software programs, and then import it back into Pro Tools, and no one will notice (if you do it carefully)!

14. If students are adept, they can try and record their own vocal (although this topic is covered mainly in Module Four) and then attempt to fix specific vocal pitch issues using the Melodyne or Auto-Tune plug-ins.

Module Three:
Introduction to MIDI and Instrument Tracks

Overview/Time Allocation

See student learning outcomes below. This third module is geared toward using Pro Tools as a MIDI sequencer, without using audio tracks. It introduces students to how to create and manipulate MIDI data, and explains how MIDI differs from audio in certain respects. The virtual synthesizers provided in Pro Tools (Xpand2 and Structure) will be used. There is a MIDI-based assignment. Allow between 10 and 15 classes of 90 minutes each to complete this module.

Topics Covered

1. What is MIDI and how is it generated?

2. MIDI signal path and virtual instruments

3. Creating music in a MIDI track/Instrument track

4. Quantization of data/viewing and editing events

5. Time, tempo, and event operations

6. MIDI real-time controls (control change info)

7. Using the Xpand2 and Structure interfaces

8. Rendering MIDI data as audio

9. Transferring MIDI data to other programs

Skills Acquisition Tutorial Videos

The following movies include the skills you need: have students watch them one at a time, practice each one, and then move on to the assignment.

19. Creating a MIDI or Instrument track

20. Virtual instrument sounds in Pro Tools

21. The Xpand2 and Structure interfaces

22. Recording MIDI data and quantizing

23. Editing MIDI data (different views of data)

24. Time, tempo, and event operations

25. MIDI control change information

26. Rendering MIDI data as audio

27. Import/export of MIDI data

Prior Knowledge (Theory/Experience)

Students should have completed Modules One and Two, and they should review the textbook references and tutorial movies given with this module before undertaking the procedures and assignment.

Shortcuts to Know

Please refer to the shortcuts page at the end of the Introduction. Ensure that students attempt each shortcut, and start using as many as possible. Test students on these shortcuts at the end of each module.

Golden Rules to Know

1. When working with MIDI, creating a click track is essential—you can set this up as a default in the Pro Tools preferences settings.

2. MIDI or Instrument tracks should be set to *ticks* rather than *samples*, so if you change the tempo of your song the MIDI information will follow.

3. Work in Grid mode in general and set your grid and nudge values carefully.

4. Double-click on a MIDI region to edit it (this opens a MIDI editor window; you can choose which of these windows opens in the Pro Tools preferences).

5. Bear in mind that for playback of Pro Tools' internal sounds, you must create an Instrument track, not a MIDI track.

6. There are three windows that allow you to view MIDI data (the MIDI editor, score editor, and MIDI event list). You can also have multiple windows open at once if you wish.

7. Editing MIDI data is easier from one of these three specialized windows.

8. Note the difference between *Region* view and *Notes* view with MIDI data.

9. Note that you can open additional windows to view things like velocity—these can be found on the far left of the main Edit window, where the track color is viewable.

10. Remember that MIDI volume works rather differently from audio volume.

11. Don't confuse velocity with volume, in terms of MIDI data.

12. Remember that MIDI data is a series of events or instructions sent to a receiving device (such as a virtual instrument), and is treated and edited differently from soundwaves.

13. You may want to consider setting up an Input Quantize value, or leave quantization for later—be aware of your choices.

14. Don't forget that you can slow down the tempo of your song very easily while you're recording MIDI data, and then speed it up later, making it much easier to play complex things. MIDI will not become distorted in any way when you do this, and this kind of editing is much easier using MIDI data than audio data.

Textbook References

Both of Michael Hewitt's books (see Introduction) have plenty of information on how to work with MIDI. His *Music Theory* book explains how specific music might look when displayed as MIDI data, while the *Composition* book details how to write specific types of music in MIDI format (chapters 3–5 and 7–9).

Marc Schonbrun's *Everything Guide to Digital Home Recording* has an excellent introductory chapter on the basics of MIDI, which would be a good starting point for students.

Example Sessions, Audio, MIDI or Video Data to Use

No example files are required for this module, although a sample Pro Tools session with four or five Instrument tracks in it is included for reference.

Free Additional Resources Available

If you want to find MIDI files online, you can usually locate (via various websites) a MIDI file of every major piece of music ever written. However, note the legal and copyright issues relating to music that has not yet entered the public domain—see the Introduction for more details.

Other Materials/Equipment Needed

A MIDI keyboard or MIDI instrument is pretty much vital for this module. See the Introduction for more details about available choices in this area, and note that you don't need to have a keyboard with its own sounds—all the MIDI sounds you need can be generated by Pro Tools if you use Instrument tracks rather than MIDI tracks.

Procedures

1. Provide an overview of the module.

2. Review the key topics that will be covered.

3. Start by explaining the basics of MIDI (see textbook references).

4. Explain some of the history behind MIDI (invented as a protocol in 1983, etc).

5. Explain that MIDI is a set of instructions that are received by a device such as a synthesizer or soundcard. You can think of it as a 16-lane highway in which data flows down each MIDI channel.

6. Play some examples of MIDI sequencing in released or famous records (perhaps something from the band Scritti Politti's *Cupid and Psyche* record). Choose groundbreaking records that demonstrated sequencing and MIDI for the first time. Other examples could be Donna Summer's "I Feel Love" or Frankie Goes to Hollywood's *Welcome to the Pleasuredome*.

7. Open the MIDI sequencing example that comes with the lesson plans.

8. Why does the data look different from audio?

9. Can it be edited and manipulated in a different way than audio?

10. Have students watch tutorial videos 19–27, and as usual, after watching each video, practice what they have learned.

11. In particular, take time to play with the Xpand2 and Structure interfaces (movie #21) (see **Figs. 6** and **7**), as these are really going to be the core of what students will use for MIDI data, and both provide great depth and sophistication. Xpand2 allows you to extensively modify its considerable list of sounds, and also allows layering of sounds along with including an arpeggiator and effects.

Fig. 6

Fig. 7

12. If time is available, have students also explore other virtual instruments in Pro Tools 8, such as the excellent Hammond organ simulator, called DB-33, as well as the Boom or BFD Lite drum simulation plug-ins. Bear in mind that if you have a MIDI keyboard with knobs on it, it can be used to control the virtual knobs in any of the virtual instruments by right-clicking (Control-clicking if you have a one-button Mac mouse) on any knob you see on the screen, and choosing Learn MIDI CC, then turning the real knob on the MIDI keyboard. This can be very creative and lead to very different sounds being developed.

13. It is important to have a discussion on whether or not to quantize MIDI data. For certain kinds of music, some MIDI data works much better if it is heavily quantized, and some MIDI data will sound way too mechanical if quantized. Also consider whether to enable Input Quantize, where Pro Tools automatically quantizes your data.

14. Students should also start to work with the shortcuts (see Introduction).

15. Once students have reviewed the tutorial videos sufficiently and practiced the skills they will need to employ, review the golden rules.

16. Students should then do their assignments (below). Allow time for students to play and comment on each other's assignments.

17. Evaluate the assessment criteria for all students; they can start by assessing themselves.

18. Review extension topics for those students who are ready and able to move on.

Student Assignment Details

The assignment for this module is to create a song containing four or more Instrument tracks. Students should choose a different timbre for each track, and at least one should have some effects added to it from inside the Xpand2 window.

Note: If you have a MIDI keyboard with its own onboard sounds connected to Pro Tools, you can use these sounds for the assignment, but bear in mind that the audio in this case will be generated by the keyboard, so students will need to plug their headphones into the keyboard and create a MIDI track rather than an Instrument track in Pro Tools. If you prefer not to do this, you can still use the keyboard, just turn the keyboard volume down and use the sound from the Pro Tools Instrument track (this will typically come through the Mbox audio output).

Should students wish to write drum parts using MIDI, they should probably use the Structure software synthesizer rather than Xpand2, since it is more dedicated to drum programming.

Also note that for each track, you must create a different instance of Xpand2 in the mixer, and this *may* start causing memory delays on your computer (depending on how much RAM you have). If that is the case, you may wish to render some of the MIDI data as actual audio. If you're in the middle of working on a Pro Tools MIDI sequence, this is probably best done by taking the following steps:

1. Save the work.

2. Mute any tracks that you don't wish to render as audio.

3. Play your sequence to make sure you're hearing just the tracks you want to render.

4. Bounce the song (File>Bounce To>Disc), and choose *stereo interleaved.*

5. Save the audio file to a memorable location.

6. Import that same file back into Pro Tools (it will automatically create a new stereo audio track of what you bounced).

7. Check that it sounds OK (solo it and play the session).

8. Delete the old Instrument tracks from your session, so they no longer use system resources.

9. Your newly rendered audio will now play along with your remaining Instrument tracks.

Students should also have learned how to quantize MIDI data, as well as edit it, transpose it, repeat it, and nudge it.

Assessment/Learning Outcomes

Students should be able to:

1. Understand the history and basics of MIDI and MIDI data

2. Create Instrument or MIDI tracks in Pro Tools

3. Work with the Xpand2/Structure interfaces and edit sounds

4. Create and edit MIDI data

5. Import MIDI data from an external source

6. Understand quantization of data

7. Work with different views of MIDI data (piano roll/notation)

8. Understand MIDI velocity and control change information

9. Explain the difference between MIDI and audio data

10. Render MIDI or Instrument tracks as audio

11. Know all the Pro Tools shortcuts listed above

12. Share and describe what they have done in their assignments

Extension Topics (If Required)

A good extension task is to take a MIDI file from an online source such as www.prs. net (free to join; thousands of MIDI files of classical music available), download it, and import it into Pro Tools. See tutorial movie #27.

Once the MIDI file has been imported into a new Pro Tools session, students can create a number of Instrument tracks in Pro Tools and then drag the data from each of the MIDI channels/tracks into a new Instrument track (then delete the old MIDI tracks, which are no longer needed).

Students can choose appropriate sounds in Xpand2 or Structure (or any of the other virtual instruments supplied with Pro Tools) to arm each Instrument track, edit the MIDI data if need be, make changes to the speed and key of the file, perhaps add some effects into the Xpand2 player, and bounce the resulting session to a stereo audio file.

Module Four: Recording New Audio

Overview/Time Allocation

See student learning outcomes below. This fourth module is designed to help students start recording their own music straight into Pro Tools, with all the challenges that this may bring. Students should create several tracks of audio and learn to balance what is currently being recorded with what has already been recorded. There is an audio recording assignment, but the art of mixing will be covered in the next module. Allow between 10 and 15 classes of 90 minutes each to complete this module.

Topics Covered

1. Using microphones—types of mics
2. Microphone placement
3. Signal levels/signal path/monitoring
4. Overdubbing and dropping in/out
5. Takes/creating a track from different takes (compositing)
6. Engineering someone else's session

Skills Acquisition Tutorial Videos

The following movies include the skills you need: have students watch them one at a time, practice each one, and then move on to the assignment.

28. Setting up a track to record (monitoring)
29. Working with MIDI and audio in the same session
30. Overdubbing/drop-in recording
31. Using different takes (track compositing)

Prior Knowledge (Theory/Experience)

Students should have completed Modules One through Three, and should review the textbook references and tutorial movies with this module before undertaking the procedures and assignment.

Shortcuts to Know

Please refer to the shortcuts page at the end of the Introduction. Ensure that students attempt each shortcut, and start using as many as possible. Test students on these shortcuts at the end of each module.

Golden Rules to Know

► Never go into the red when you record!
► Be aware of latency issues when monitoring signals.

► Establish a clear, concise workflow in your mind when recording.

► Understand the pre-roll options in Pro Tools.

► Understand loop record in Pro Tools.

Textbook References

For information on the basics of digital audio, I recommend the updated *Everything Guide to Digital Home Recording* by Marc Schonbrun, chapters 5 and 6.

You can also locate good articles online about digital audio, sample rates, sample resolution, bit depth, and the Nyquist Theorem by searching for any of these terms. Students should be somewhat familiar with all of these terms, and be able to describe what they mean in plain English. Harry Nyquist is the man who determined the bandwidth requirements for transmitting information in 1928.

For information about types of microphones and techniques for setting up microphones for recording, read chapter 9 of the *Everything Guide to Digital Home Recording* book.

Example Sessions, Audio, MIDI, or Video Data to Use

If you'd like students to hear an example of a model assignment, they could listen to some of the multitrack sessions for Module Five, since many of these include a mixture of real tracks (guitar/vocal/keyboard) and looped tracks (drums, in most cases).

Guitarists who want to plug their guitars straight into Pro Tools can use virtual amplifier simulator plug-ins. An obvious choice is Eleven Free, which ships with Pro Tools 8. To use it, create an audio track in Pro Tools and connect a guitar to your Mbox or audio interface. Then go to the mixer in Pro Tools and insert Eleven Free from Plug-ins>Harmonic>Eleven Free (mono). From here you can audition various amps and cabinets from within the Eleven plug-in. The guitar track needs to be record-enabled, and you may wish to mix the level of the clean guitar being sent to Pro Tools with the effected signal coming back from Pro Tools, using the Mix pot on the front of the Mbox. Bear in mind that in this setup you're not actually recording the effected signal. You're hearing the effect because the plug-in is inserted. You can change the settings later on the plug-in without having to re-record your guitar track.

Free Additional Resources Available

Since this module requires students to record their own music, external resources are not really appropriate beyond the use of the drum and other various loops that students can use (included free in Pro Tools 8 with the Big Fish Audio loops).

Other Materials/Equipment Needed

1. Microphones (dynamic or condenser)

2. Musical instruments

3. Cables to connect the audio source to the interface

4. (Optional) Guitar preamp/amp-modeling device

Procedures

1. Discuss the goals for this module and the topics that will be covered.

2. Start by talking about digital recording theory.

3. What are the components of a digital recording?

4. The sample rate and the sample depth (or bit resolution)?

5. See the textbook references for more details on this important topic. Students should understand what is actually happening when they press the Record button and start to play.

6. Next, explain how to set up for recording, and why a digital recording shouldn't go into the red. In analog recording, fully saturating the magnetic tape may produce a pleasing sound, but not so with digital distortion, or clipping. Here you want to record a clean signal that you can later make louder using various techniques.

7. Have students watch the tutorial videos and practice starting a new session in Pro Tools, setting up a new track, monitoring the signal, and getting a decent sound.

8. Once students have sufficiently reviewed the tutorial videos and practiced the skills they will need to employ, review the golden rules.

9. Students should also be using the shortcuts (see Introduction).

10. Now, bearing in mind the assignment for this module, pair students who don't play an instrument with those who do, as the assignment will

require a live instrument track to be recorded—ideally guitar or another acoustic instrument.

11. One of the big factors students will encounter is the latency experienced when recording live. *Latency* is the difference in time between hearing the signal being sent to Pro Tools and hearing the same signal coming back from Pro Tools. This can be ignored entirely by muting the output of the track when recording (so you only hear the signal being sent to Pro Tools, along with the other tracks already recorded), but this may not work if you want to use the plug-ins in Pro Tools. If you are using the latest 3rd generation Mbox, you may find that latency is lower, and you will not find it necessary to mute the track into which you are recording.

12. Guitarists who wish to record electric guitar have two choices: 1) use an amp and set up the exact sound they want, then mic the amp and attempt to capture their sound live; or 2) (a much less intrusive option in a classroom, where students will probably be recording with headphones) learn how to add guitar effects inside Pro Tools. This way students effectively send a clean signal from their guitar into Pro Tools, add an effect (which can be changed later), and hear *that* signal coming back when they record.

13. The best way of achieving this is to use the Eleven plug-in, which simulates guitar preamps and cabinets digitally. First, students create a new blank session in Pro Tools. Then they add a click track or import drum loops at the correct speed to match the feel of the song to be created (these can be swapped out later, but the speed of the song should definitely be established at this stage). This is a critical lesson to learn. Students should work in Grid mode and set Pro Tools to the same speed as the drum loop(s) they are using.

14. Students then create a new audio track for the guitar. Plug an electric guitar into the Mbox, go to the Mixer in Pro Tools, and insert the Eleven plug-in from plug-in>Harmonic>Eleven Free (mono). Make sure this plug-in has been loaded on their machines—it ships free with Pro Tools 8.

15. Experiment with what can be achieved with this plug-in—note that students may need to record-enable their guitar track in order to hear the signal coming back from Pro Tools. They will also need to calibrate the settings on their Mbox carefully: there are monitor and mix controls on the front of the Mbox, and these will make all the difference in ensuring that students hear a mix of what is being sent to Pro Tools

clean and what is coming back from Pro Tools effected. As with step 11 above, those using the 3rd generation Mbox will find that latency issues are lessened, and the mix/monitor knob has been removed due to low latency with this device.

16. Students who don't play electric guitar can explore setting up a microphone and recording an acoustic instrument. Keyboard players can attempt to mic up a real piano, or (if you have a keyboard with onboard sounds) they could plug the output of the keyboard into Pro Tools and explore the plug-ins inside the Mix window.

17. Students should definitely experiment with using effects on their live track before recording it. After recording their live track, they can go back and alter the plug-in settings for the track *without having to re-record it.*

18. Take time to explore with students Pro Tools' track compositing/comping feature (see tutorial movie #31 on this). Students should learn how to set locate points in Pro Tools, turn on the loop-record feature, and record multiple takes of the same track that they can later piece together to create the perfect take. Ensure that students are competent at this before they start their official assignment.

19. Review the assignment. Have the class listen to the session examples that come with this guide so students can get a feel for what they are being asked to create.

20. Students should also create at least one Instrument track for this assignment, so make sure they have effectively completed Module Three on MIDI/Instrument tracks (and how to use Xpand2 and Structure) before attempting this module.

21. Also make sure that students understand how to select audio loops from the Big Fish Audio library, as these can also be used on this assignment.

22. Allow time for students to play and comment upon each other's assignments.

23. Evaluate the assessment criteria for all students; they can start by assessing themselves.

24. Review extension topics for those students who are ready and able to move on.

Student Assignment Details

The assignment for Module Four is similar to that for Module Three.

Using live audio and a mixture of drum loops and Instrument tracks, create a multitrack session with at least four tracks in it, at least one of which must be recorded live by plugging an instrument into the audio interface or by using a microphone. The live recorded track(s) should then be edited and have effects added.

Other tracks can be created by importing audio from the Big Fish Audio loops that come with Pro Tools. It might be a good idea to start by first selecting and importing drum loops to make a backing track, and then begin recording live instruments to play along with these loops. Students will need to understand elastic audio and the workspace window (Modules One and Two) if they are to do this part of the assignment effectively.

For those not using Pro Tools 8, or for those who do not have the Big Fish Audio loops, you may be able to download some audio loops from the Internet, or consider purchasing an inexpensive drum loop library, such as those available from Sony.

The finished song should have several different instruments in it (for example, drums, bass, guitar, other instruments, and/or live vocals), and should be mixed/bounced to a stereo file.

Those who have attempted to balance audio levels and use effects on their tracks should be given a higher score. The song should be a maximum of 3 minutes in length.

Assessment/Learning Outcomes

Students should be able to:

1. Understand different microphones
2. Understand different mic placement techniques
3. Record audio straight into Pro Tools
4. Record multiple tracks into Pro Tools

5. Overdub tracks in Pro Tools

6. Work with track compositing in Pro Tools

7. Know all the Pro Tools shortcuts listed above

8. Share and describe what they have done in their assignments

Extension Topics (If Required)

Students can engineer each other's recording sessions, and establish clearly defined roles as engineer and producer (looking ahead to Modules Five and Six).

Establish clear ground rules up front, such as the ensemble to be recorded as well as the time, venue, and length of the recording session, so that students become aware of the real-world challenges engineers face in capturing high-quality audio in a limited time period. They should also experiment with adding overdubs to each other's sessions by acting as guest musicians on another student's session.

Try recording the school choir or school band, perhaps using a stereo microphone setup with a regular Mbox, or using a multiple microphone setup going into a mixing board (and from there, having a stereo output into the Mbox). Examples of a good stereo microphone pair for recording ensembles live in concert or rehearsal would be:

- M-Audio Pulsar II Matched Pair (educational price around $300; www.m-audio.com/products/en_us/PulsarIIMatchedPair.html)
- Crown Audio SASS-P MK II (Pressure Zone microphone with stereo output; www.crownaudio.com)

Module Five: Learning to Mix— Working in a Multitrack Environment

Overview/Time Allocation

See student learning outcomes below. This fifth module is designed for students to act as audio engineers/producers, primarily working with preexisting material, perhaps created by someone else. The art of mixing is introduced, as well as some mastering principles. There is a mixdown assignment to be completed. Allow between 10 and 15 classes of 90 minutes each to complete this module.

Topics Covered

1. More about the signal path (creating an auxiliary return)

2. Creating different mixes of the same song

3. Grouping tracks

4. Automating the mixdown—recording/drawing fader movements

5. More on using EQ, compression, and reverb

6. Using AudioSuite to render audio

7. Using delay and more advanced effects

8. Adding a master fader

9. Mastering the track as a stereo mix

Skills Acquisition Tutorial Videos

The following movies include the skills you need: have students watch them one at a time, practice each one, and then move on to the assignment.

32. Navigating a multitrack session

33. Grouping tracks together

34. Creating an auxiliary input for reverb

35. Recording fader movements

36. Using AudioSuite

37. Adding a master fader

38. Mastering tools for the final mix

Prior Knowledge (Theory/Experience)

Students should have completed Modules One through Four, and they should review the textbook references and tutorial movies for this module before undertaking the procedures and assignment.

Shortcuts to Know

Please refer to the shortcuts page at the end of the Introduction. Ensure that students attempt each shortcut, and start using as many as possible. Test students on these shortcuts at the end of each module.

Golden Rules to Know

1. If the mixer is getting crowded, use the narrow mix window view.

2. Group tracks together to make mixing easier.

3. Some effects are not meant to be inserts; some effects only work properly as inserts.

4. Use delay creatively to fill out the sound of a track.

5. Delay works very effectively when it is in sync with the speed of your session.

6. Understand how to calculate delay times in milliseconds, working out how long each beat of your song is in milliseconds.

7. Save computer memory by rendering some audio before mixdown: bounce effected tracks to disk and reimport them as audio (these then won't require any effects to be added).

8. Mixing a song is much more than simply moving faders around.

9. Have a good reference recording on hand to compare your mix to.

Textbook References

It is important to make sure that students understand the audio *signal path*—specifically, when to use insert effects and when to use auxiliary send/returns. Review chapters 10 and 15–17 of the *Everything Guide to Digital Home Recording* book. These topics should have been covered previously in Module Two, but a refresher is always a good idea.

For mixing basics (and also some information about *mastering*, which isn't covered a great deal in these resources), read chapter 15 of *Everything* (chapter 17 in the new edition), as well as chapter 19 of the Hewitt book *Composition for Computer Musicians*.

Example Sessions, Audio, MIDI, or Video Data to Use

Various multitrack sessions are included for students to use with this module. Note that these are Pro Tools sessions rather than raw audio; the actual session file (the .ptf file) that you open in Pro Tools is linked to several other folders that contain the audio and fade information. Be sure to copy all the folders onto your computer or hard disk.

Free Additional Resources Available

It probably won't be easy to find downloadable multitrack audio for students to use, so plenty is provided in this module. If you do know a local recording studio, it may be worth inquiring whether they have any outtakes students could experiment with—but bear in mind that you need multiple tracks of audio for this module, not just a stereo track.

Also, look online for Eagle Rock Entertainment's excellent *Classic Album Series*, comprising about 20 documentaries exploring the making of such groundbreaking albums as:

- *Electric Ladyland* by Jimi Hendrix
- *Rumors* by Fleetwood Mac
- *Graceland* by Paul Simon
- *Songs in the Key of Life* by Stevie Wonder
- *The Joshua Tree* by U2
- *Dark Side of the Moon* by Pink Floyd

Some of these are available as used DVDs at Amazon.com (www.amazon.com/gp/series/215?ref_=pd_serl_dvd&edition=dvd&page=1). You may also be able to find excerpts of this series on YouTube.

What is so great about these documentaries is that they contain the original multitrack tapes, with the actual artists and engineers explaining the exact techniques they used in the making of the records. Students will pick up an amazing amount of information by watching any of the documentaries in this series.

Other Materials/Equipment Needed

No additional materials are needed, although for final mixes, it is highly desirable to hear the playback through actual speakers rather than headphones. In the audio industry it would be unheard of to do a professional mix using only headphones. See the Introduction for suggestions about speakers.

Also (and this is strictly optional), in many Pro Tools environments engineers use a control surface for mixing such as the Project Mix from M-Audio, or the Digi 003 Factory or Command 8 from Avid all the way up to their excellent Control 24. This hardware allows you to control all the actions of the onscreen mixer using real faders and knobs, so it is something of a throwback to the days of mixing with an analog mixer, except that these control surfaces are simply controlling the software inside Pro Tools. Students should experience using controllers at some stage. At the top end of this genre, you have the Icon and Venue consoles from Avid, which may be worth checking out online so students can see the connection between where they're at in the classroom and where they would be in the pro audio industry. The software is almost identical—it's just that the hardware gets more expensive!

Procedures

1. Review the goals of this module.

2. Review the textbook references, and explore the relatively recent history of multitrack recording. Watch any of the DVDs in the *Classic Albums* series (see Free Resources above).

3. In the past, most songs were recorded live to a stereo master, until the advent of 4-track, 8-track, and 16-track tape recorders made it possible to start multitracking music. Research the development of this technology. Include the (again, quite recent) period when artists stopped using tape recorders and started doing multitrack recording on their computers instead—what prompted this change?

4. Discuss with students how multitrack technology could radically alter the process of composing and recording. What things would be different about the process, compared with simply recording live in the studio?

5. An obvious example of existing or famous music to listen to would be *Tubular Bells* by Mike Oldfield from the early 1970s, where he played all the tracks himself one by one. Another example would be any CD by Pink Floyd after *Dark Side of the Moon*. Pink Floyd were notoriously

slow at making records—taking six months to make a CD was unheard of before the mid-1970s.

6. Listen to an outstandingly well-mixed CD like *The Seeds of Love* by Tears for Fears from the late 1980s. Ask students to listen carefully (perhaps with headphones) and detail what they hear in the finished mix. How many tracks are there? Watch the video for the title track—compare it to the Beatles' *Sgt. Pepper's Lonely Hearts Club Band*.

7. Talk about the separation of tracks that happens in a multitrack recording, and the ability to process every track in a different way. (Hence the need to devote significant time to mixing a song.)

8. Review the topics that need to be covered; in particular the need to start using auxiliary sends/returns (see textbook references) and also how to group tracks to make mixing easier and use up less computer resources.

9. Watch the tutorial movies, and make sure students spend time practicing the techniques before attempting the student assignment. In particular, students should be able to create an auxiliary send/return for reverb, as effects such as reverb should not be used as inserts in a mixer track. Discuss why you should use an auxiliary send/return for reverb, and why effects like EQ or compression should be used as insert effects instead. The textbooks will help in this regard.

10. Several songs are provided with this module for students to use. These are unmixed multitrack Pro Tools session files that are ready to be worked on. If students have already created a multitrack song as part of Module Five, they could use that, but you should definitely focus on songs containing over eight tracks of audio.

11. Students should also be using the shortcuts (see Introduction).

12. Once students have viewed the tutorial videos and practiced the skills they will need to employ, review the golden rules.

13. When you are confident that students are ready, have them attempt the assignment. Note that it might be appropriate for them to pair up for their first mix, since they will have to make many choices about EQ, reverb, delay, compression, levels and other plug-ins they may wish to explore.

14. Allow time for students to play and comment upon each other's assignments.

15. Evaluate the assessment criteria for all students; they can start by assessing themselves.

16. Review extension topics for those students who are ready and able to move on.

Student Assignment Details

1. Choose one of the multitrack sessions included with these lessons, and mix it down to a final stereo mix. There is a great deal of creative scope within this assignment: the choice of EQ and effects, the choice of levels, and whether or not to include certain tracks in the mix.

2. Students should focus on key effects (EQ, reverb, compression), and try some delay on certain tracks. They should definitely be creating auxiliary sends, for reverb in particular, and try not to maximize the computer's memory by running too many effects.

3. They should also try using AudioSuite to render some track effects, perhaps saving memory, and save final work that might need to be done in the mix.

4. Lastly, students should demonstrate that they know how to create groups for some of their tracks, as well as a master fader. Students should also use some level of automation in the final mix (for example, adding fades on certain tracks, recording the fader movements on certain tracks or groups, and adding automation to the master fader volume by drawing a volume curve onto that track (shown in the relevant tutorial movie).

5. It may be appropriate for students to work in pairs at this stage, since this is a major assignment.

Assessment/Learning Outcomes

Students should be able to:

1. Understand the concept of an auxiliary send/return

2. Choose appropriate effects for a multitrack mixdown

3. Know how to group tracks together

4. Create a master fader and send the outputs of all the tracks to it

5. Perform global editing functions

6. Work with AudioSuite in Pro Tools

7. Stay within the memory limits of their computer

8. Create a final stereo mix that represents the song accurately

9. Know all the Pro Tools shortcuts listed above

10. Share and describe what they have done in their assignments

Extension Topics (If Required)

There are two suggested extension tasks:

1. Students can try to remix another of the sessions in the accompanying files, following the same steps as in the regular assignment.

2. Students can try a more radical remix of one of the multitrack sessions by importing a different set of loops from the Big Fish Audio collection and matching them to the tempo of the song using elastic time. Then they can remove or mute various aspects of the existing session, and alter the tone or feel of the session entirely. They can then render this as a completed mix with the appropriate effects applied to the tracks. They might also edit the existing session into a shorter song, perhaps for potential radio play (a common engineering task in the music industry).

Module Six: Working with Video and Creating Film/TV Soundtracks

Overview/Time Allocation

See student learning outcomes below. This final module brings together multiple media (audio, MIDI, and video) and leads to a final project. Students learn about the constituent parts that make up a TV program, documentary, or movie, and how to manipulate these elements to render a completed movie with its own soundtrack. There are two assignments—creating the music and voiceover for a nature documentary, and creating the backing track for a 30-second Hollywood movie trailer. Allow between 15 and 20 classes of 90 minutes each to complete this module.

Topics Covered

1. Finding videos and importing them

2. Looking at hit points/time code

3. Writing a voiceover script

4. Recording/editing voiceover

5. Strip Silence feature for voiceovers

6. Adding an audio soundtrack

7. Creating sound effects using Xpand2

8. Mixing elements together

9. Bouncing to a QuickTime movie

10. Video codecs for posting on the Internet/podcasts

Skills Acquisition Tutorial Videos

The following movies include the skills you need: have students watch them one at a time, practice each one, and then move on to the assignment.

39. Importing a movie and adding marker points

40. Working with Strip Silence for a voiceover track

41. Rendering a QuickTime movie, and different movie codecs

Prior Knowledge (Theory/Experience)

Students should have completed Modules One through Five, and should review the textbook references and tutorial movies with this module before undertaking the procedures and assignment.

Shortcuts to Know

Please refer to the shortcuts page at the end of the Introduction. Ensure that students attempt each shortcut, and use as many as possible. Test students on these shortcuts at the end of each module.

Golden Rules to Know

1. Listen to great examples of film and TV music.

2. Note how little dialogue is used in many movies—the music creates the mood.

3. The most important question for a film composer to ask is: Does it fit the picture?

4. Be ready to explore many different genres of music—some of which will be far outside your comfort zone.

5. Don't crowd the dialogue with too much music.

6. Choose sound effects wisely.

Textbook References

It may be hard to find low-cost or accessible textbook resources on how to compose for film and video. You might be able to locate video footage of film composers talking about their techniques. The best option would be to invite a film composer to your class as a guest speaker. The technology for composing for video is fairly new, and you should explore lectures or clinics given by composers for video games (a whole world in itself), TV, and film.

Key composers whose music you may wish to investigate include:

- Alf Clausen (*The Simpsons*)
- Howard Shore (*Lord of the Rings* and many other movies)
- Danny Elfman (*Batman* and many other movies)
- Thomas Newman (*The Shawshank Redemption, The Green Mile,* and others)
- Scott Bradley (*Tom & Jerry* cartoons and much more)
- Carl Stalling (many cartoons of the 1940s and '50s)
- Henry Mancini ("*The Pink Panther* Theme" and others)
- John Williams (a huge number of movies over the past 40 years)
- Michael Kamen (film composer who also orchestrated the music of Metallica)
- Lalo Schifrin (*Mission Impossible* and many others)

Most of these composers have websites, and you may be able to locate videos of them talking about their craft. For example, *Star Wars: Episode I* contains some footage on the extras DVD of the conductor and orchestra working directly to picture.

Example Sessions, Audio, MIDI, or Video Data to Use

For this module, an example of the kind of project that students should create is included for you to play and discuss. For their assignment, students should use the free resources available (see below), as well as their own resources.

Free Additional Resources Available

For the movie trailer assignment, you should be able to download trailers from various sites, but bear in mind that these sites may have pop-up ads and other questionable content. Movie trailers should be selected carefully and downloaded by the teacher well in advance. Try twww.empiremovies.com/trailers, or www.movie-list.com/classics-alpha.php. The latter site allows you to click on a movie and easily download the trailer in a variety of formats. QuickTime is the best format to choose (look for files ending in .mov). For thousands of free videos that are education friendly, go to www.archive.org. It's the best available resource.

If you are looking to download a movie from YouTube (www.youtube.com), be warned: this is not a trivial process, and you need to be aware of whether you might be contravening copyright. YouTube uses the FLV video format, and you will need additional software to convert the YouTube link into a format Pro Tools can read by default, such as a QuickTime movie. Do an online search for "convert YouTube movie" to find out more about these resources.

You might also want to buy QuickTime Pro for basic video editing ($30); this gives you the option to convert (transcode) certain movie formats, and compress a movie down so it is easier to share with others.

Also download Handbrake from www.handbrake.fr–this is an excellent free application that allows you to "rip" a DVD that you put into your computer's hard drive and render it as a QuickTime movie. It will allow you to choose lots of formats/codecs for the resultant movie, and makes the process of getting video off a DVD a painless experience. Try and observe copyright laws!

Other Materials/Equipment Needed

For the extension tasks, having either a Flip Video camera or a handheld audio recorder like the M-Audio Microtrack II or Zoom H2 (or a variety of others) is desirable. Consult a decent music technology retailer for suggestions.

Procedures

1. Review the goals of this module and the topics that will be covered.

2. By this stage, students should be able to work in Pro Tools without too much direct guidance from the teacher. If they are still lacking a few skills or specific knowledge, perhaps review the appropriate tutorial videos from the previous modules.

3. Having students discuss and analyze good examples of film scores and/or music for documentaries would be extremely valuable for this module.

4. Successful film and TV composers can create music in a variety of genres, so students need to widen their knowledge to encompass some classical, jazz, and world music at the very least, so they can start thinking more creatively about suitable music for the picture, be it animation, a nature documentary, or a movie trailer.

5. If students lack the ability or knowledge to create a full orchestral score for a motion picture, what instruments or sounds can they more easily use that will *sound* like a specific genre such as classical, jazz, or world music?

6. What makes a great movie score?

7. Can students name TV shows or movies whose music or theme song they like? Why do they like the theme, and why is it so closely identified with the video? Students should have developed constructive and musical terminology by this stage, and should be able to explain in some detail what is going on.

8. Obvious choices of what to look at are cartoons such as *Tom & Jerry, The Simpsons,* or *South Park,* the Planet Earth BBC/Disney nature documentary, famous TV series theme songs, and one or two good movie trailers.

9. While they watch, ask students to describe what the music is doing, as well as what the action is on the screen. You could start by turning off the sound so students only see the picture, and have to imagine the kind of soundtrack that could be employed. Short clips of 15–30 seconds might be a good starting point. An alternative would be to play only the music without the picture, so students can imagine the images before they see them.

Here are some questions to consider asking students (you may develop additional ones):

1. Is the music live or synthesized?

2. How many instruments are being used?

3. Are any special techniques used in the performance, sound, effects, or recording?

4. How does the music work with any dialogue in the movie or program?

5. How is the music balanced?

6. How much dialogue is there compared with picture?

7. How would you go about designing the music for that same documentary, TV program, or movie?

8. Is there a strong or memorable theme being used?

9. What is the emotion that is being conveyed by the music?

10. Can you guess what kinds of things are going on in the video, simply by hearing the music?

11. Discuss themes and motifs: Can these be ascribed to the characters in a movie, or to the emotions or the action?

12. Are there some obvious ways to generate mood or emotion through music, such as major/minor, fast/slow, high-pitched/low pitched/timbre?

13. Before students start on their assignments, have them watch the tutorial movies and practice some of the techniques.

14. Review available materials (including free resources and included files).

15. At this stage, you might review with students any movies you may have downloaded that will be useful for the assignment—movie trailers, silent movies, voiceover audio, etc.

16. Review any textbook references.

17. Review golden rules and shortcuts that should be used by the class.

18. Explain the assignment: establish the timelines and how you will assess completed projects.

19. Allow time for students to play and comment upon each other's assignments.

20. Evaluate the assessment criteria for all students; they can start by assessing themselves.

21. Review extension topics for those students who are ready and able to move on.

Student Assignment Details

There are two suggested projects to complete: think of these as possible final projects for the whole course, since this is the final module, and students should draw upon multiple skills in order to complete these assignments.

Assignment One

1. Create a nature documentary. Find or record a movie about a specific topic relating to nature. Cut it down to a maximum of 3 minutes, then import the movie into an empty Pro Tools session.

2. Write voiceover text and record/edit it on its own audio track, so there is a strong narrative, but allow space between for music to be added.

3. Create any extra tracks you need, and then record a soundtrack using a mixture of audio (real instruments you have recorded) and MIDI Instrument data (using Xpand2 or Structure). Render as a QuickTime movie.

Assignment Two

1. Take an existing movie trailer (see Free Resources) for an action movie. Retain the voiceover (by carefully editing the audio track for the trailer), but remove any music, and add a new soundtrack that includes drum loops, music, and sound effects appropriate to what is happening on the screen.

2. The trailer may contain numerous jump cuts between different camera angles, etc. It should be a maximum of 90 seconds long. Render as a QuickTime movie.

3. Students can use Xpand2 or Structure on Instrument tracks, but they should be careful not to create too many instances of Xpand2 in the same song or the computer may run out of memory. In such instances, they should *render* one or more of the Xpand2 tracks as an audio track (follow the steps given in Module Three's student assignment).

4. Students should also create at least one audio track from scratch and record something using a microphone and instrument, or plug in a guitar or a keyboard with sounds (if one if available). They can also import loops from the Big Fish Audio loops folders.

Assessment/Learning Outcomes

Students should be able to:

1. Import a video and add marker points that match the action

2. Create a sound effects track (using Xpand2 or Structure)

3. Write and record/edit a voiceover track

4. Create a musical soundtrack for the video

5. Use automation to balance the different tracks

6. Render the project as a QuickTime movie

7. Be aware of other techniques composers use (5.1 surround sound, etc.)

8. Know all the Pro Tools shortcuts listed above

9. Share and describe what they have done in their assignments

Extension Topics (If Required)

There are two suggested extension tasks.

1. Students can film their own movie and add a soundtrack to it. Inexpensive video cameras are available (check out www.theflip.com) for students to easily produce their own basic movies. They should edit their movie before importing it into Pro Tools. iMovie (for Mac users) might be the best software for doing this. Windows users can use Pinnacle Studio (see Introduction for details about video software resources).

2. An alternative extension task leads into broadcast journalism: Have students choose a topic and interview people for the voiceover soundtrack (recording the conversations with a microphone straight into Pro Tools, or with a handheld portable digital recorder). They can then grab some video footage of the topic they're covering, and put the two together. Lastly, they can add a musical soundtrack and/or sound effects for the background, and render the project in Pro Tools as a QuickTime movie.

About the Author

Robin Hodson is the Mid-Atlantic Manager for SoundTree, based in Baltimore. He comes from a musical family; his grandfather founded a symphony orchestra and music conservatory in Zimbabwe, and his mother taught music for 50 years. An accomplished composer and performer, working in a variety of differing genres, Robin is also a recording engineer, songwriter, and arranger.

Robin received his master's degree at Magdalen College, Oxford, before moving to the United States in 1999. He worked for Sibelius/Avid for 13 years, training students at universities and schools all over the US and Canada in how to use Avid music technology products, before he joined SoundTree in the summer of 2009. Robin has also authored several free quick-start guides and videos on how to use Sibelius's Groovy Music.

Visit the author's websites at:

www.robinhodson.com

http://members.sibeliusmusic.com/robinhodson